MEMOIR OF A VICTORIAN ANTIQUARIAN

Edited by

SCOTT A. MCLEAN

Grosvenor House
Publishing Limited

This book is published by
Grosvenor House Publishing Ltd
Link House
140 The Broadway, Tolworth, Surrey, KT6 7HT.
www.grosvenorhousepublishing.co.uk

A CIP record for this book
is available from the British Library

ISBN 978-1-83975-541-5

Cover Art: Depicts a sketch made by David Markham while excavating a prehistoric burial near Scarborough in 1835

Scott McLean is Director of Explore History Ltd., a company established in 2015 after 16 years teaching at Queen's University (Kingston) Bader International Study Centre at Herstmonceux Castle in East Sussex, England. He has researched and written on a wide range of topics related to British and Canadian history and has long had a passion for the discovery and analysis of primary source materials.

Also by Scott McLean

The Unusual Histories of a Curious Dog (Children's)

The Gardens of Herstmonceux: A History and Guide

Researching Your Ancestors in Simcoe County:
A Study in Migratory Patterns and Family History
(with Nancy Leveque)

William Wye Smith: Recollections of a Nineteenth Century
Scottish Canadian (with Michael Vance)

From Lochnaw to Manitoulin: A Highland Soldier's
Tour Through Upper Canada

EXPLORE HISTORY

CONTENTS

ACKNOWLEDGEMENTS

This book has been a long time in the works and would not have been possible without the continued support of many very important people. Special thanks go to Robin, who has always indulged my passion for history and put up with dusty documents littering the house. Special mention also goes out to David Bevan, with whom I worked when I first began the project, and whose encouragement and continued support has meant a great deal over the years.

LIST OF ILLUSTRATIONS

A NOTE ON THE TEXT

The following work is based upon an extensive six-volume manuscript "Memorials of David F. Markham," written sometime shorty before 1913 by his son Sir Clements R. Markham. The volumes, originally beautifully bound in leather, were found in a state of disrepair due to age and neglect, and through the removal of a series of watercolours made by David Markham during a tour through the Mediterranean. The watercolours were sold at Christies in 2004 and the volumes of text tossed aside as they were deemed to be of little value. The editor came upon them by chance at Battle Market, East Sussex, one cold winters day, and happily gave them a new home.

The author of the "Memorials" was Sir Clements Robert Markham, second son of David F. Markham on whose life the work is primarily focussed. Clements was a prolific writer with great energy. He began a career in the navy in 1844 when he was posted to the Pacific, and during which time he developed an interest in Peru and the ancient Incan Empire. In 1850-51 he was serving aboard the H.M.S. Assistance and took part in the search for Franklin's ill-fated Arctic expedition. Against his father's wishes Clements would leave the navy in pursuit of a literary career. He immediately embarked on an expedition to Peru (1852-53), where he spent his time studying the history, archaeology and language of the country. Upon his return to England in 1853 he would be forced, due to financial circumstances and the death of his father, to pursue a career in the civil service. His passion however, remained travelling and writing, and he would go on to make his mark as a geographer, explorer and writer. He served as both Secretary and President of the Royal Geographic Society and the Haklyut Society, and was the driving force behind the Discovery Expedition to the Antarctic led by Robert Scott in 1901-1904. Later in life he wished to honour his father with a written memorial, creating the following work; however in doing so provided a great deal more.

The handwriting is that of a well-educated and accomplished writer and therefore was easy to transcribe. The main challenge was the sheer volume of detail and sifting through the countless pages of genealogical charts and descriptions of ancient families related to the Markham family. The collection includes more than a hundred photos, sketches, and several maps related to a variety of subjects, but most specifically the Markham family and the places in which they lived. Much of the text is based upon David Markham's personal papers and correspondence. David Markham kept a journal of his Mediterranean tour and his daily life from 1846 until his passing in 1853. As an educated individual with the broad interests of a true antiquarian, David Markham collected and studied a broad spectrum of subjects and kept detailed notes. The author of the 'Memorials' therefore had a rich source of information upon which to draw, as well as his own personal memories of growing up in the Markham household. The manuscript therefore is written in the words of the author, Clements Markham, but draws heavily on David Markham's own writings. The editor has therefore chosen to indicate when the author is quoting David Markham by placing the text either in quotation marks, or by a block quote.

The inclusion of references was deemed to be of particular importance for the project as they are designed to provide context and allow for the inclusion of more in-depth information on many of the subjects discussed in the text. Within the manuscript the author made extensive notations in the margins and on the backs of pages, many with very detailed information. Where such information has been added in as a reference the editor has indicated this by referring to it as an "Author's Note" at the beginning of each reference. Citations created by the editor appear as a standard footnote.

In compiling the memorial the author included a wide array of genealogical charts, descriptions of significant buildings, people and places, outside of the main body of the text. Much of this material, such as David Markham's list of all the people living in Great Horkesley parish, the lists of servants they employed, and his 'visitation cycle', is of great significance to the genealogist and social historian alike. For this reason this material has been worked into a series of appendices.

Due to the length of the manuscript, with 28 chapters and over 500 pages, it was deemed to be unfeasible to include all of the material covered by the author. Instead, the 'memorial' has been divided into three sections: Early Life, Mediterranean Travels, and Later Life. In each of these sections chapters have been chosen which best reflected the life and work of David Markham, and more importantly, dealt more directly with the history of Great Horkesley, Colchester, and its environs. The section on 'Mediterranean Travels' was included as this was deemed to best reflect David Markham as an antiquarian of high social standing, and as this was a significant turning point in the lives of the Markham family. The editor hopes readers will find this approach informative and easy to follow.

INTRODUCTION

David Francis Markham was born on the 11th of March, 1800, the third son and fourth child of eight. His father, William Markham, was the eldest son of the Archbishop of York, and had served as private secretary to Warren Hastings in India. David Markham therefore grew up in a privileged position in a very well-connected family. Growing up at the family home at Becca, located on high ground to the south of the Leeds-Tadcaster road, he was well looked after and had ample opportunity to explore the surrounding countryside and acquire an education. The home included an extensive library filled with the classics and religious works, and the house was decorated with works of art from the likes of Tintoretto, Perigino, Rembrandt, Reynolds and Gainsborough. It was here at home that David Markham early on acquired an appreciation for art and the classics, something that would continue to evolve through his early education.

David was first sent to school at Doncaster at the age of eight. Through Archbishop Markham the family had a strong association with the Westminster school and it was there, at the age of thirteen, that he would continue his studies. He was forced to leave Westminster after just two years due to illness, continuing his studies under a private tutor, a Mr. Jenkins, at Thorpe Hall near Peterborough. In 1818 he had been trained sufficiently to attend Christ Church, Oxford. Here he made a name for himself, both as an oarsman and scholar, and established a wide circle of friends who would prove influential throughout his life.[1] Life at Oxford appeared to agree with David , a fact no doubt aided by the £200 a year allowance provided by his mother. He completed his studies in 1823, entering Holy Orders the same year as curate to Mr. Landon, the Vicar of Aberford.

---

[1] His list of friends would include, among many others: David Dundas; Edward Borough, later 2nd baronet; Blayney Balfour; Tom Schiffner and C.R. Pemberton.

It was during this early stage of his career that he acquired, and was able to indulge, his growing taste for travel. While on vacation from his studies in 1818 he embarked upon his first tour of the continent, visiting Brussels, Switzerland, Heidelburg, Basel, Geneva and Paris. In 1819 he took another tour, this time with his brother William, to Holland, France, Genoa, Pavia, Milan and Venice. He made a third tour in 1823, sailing from Harwich to Gottenburg, Sweden. After visiting Stockholm he travelled to Copenhagen, Frankfurt and Heidelburg before returning home via the Rhine. In 1825 he toured Scotland, and throughout his life would regularly travel to Ireland where he had relations. The impact of these travels cannot be underestimated, and must have confirmed in him a desire to study ancient history, language and culture.

In 1826 David Markham was appointed Vicar of Stillingfleet, seven miles south of York, and in the following year he received a letter from then Prime Minister George Canning that he was being made a Canon of Windsor. This position was worth between £1000 and £1500 annually, and meant that he was now financially secure and in a position to marry.[2] He married Catherine Milner in Bolton Percy church on the 30th of August 1827. A family soon followed and the Markham's settled down into a comfortable life split between Stillingfleet and Windsor.[3]

In 1832 the peaceful existence David Markham was enjoying at Stillingfleet was disrupted by a family tragedy in Ireland. The Archdeacon's eldest son Robert had entered the army in 1819 and risen to the rank of captain in the 58th regiment. On the 30th of May 1832, while on march in Ireland, he was invited to dine with the mess of the 92nd at Fermoy, of which Colonel John McDonald was in command.

---

[2] David Markham had invested much of his personal fortune of £6000 he had received when he came of age. Stillingfleet was worth £450 a year, and with Windsor bringing on average £1500 David Markham had a yearly income of £2200.

[3] David and Catherine Markham had six children: David William Christian, Dec. 25th 1828; Clements Robert, July 20th 1830; Selina Catharine Laura, August 1st 1835; Warren, July 16th 1835; Georgina Elizabeth, Dec. 15th 1838; and Gertrude Caroline Lucy, Sept. 28th 1842.

> The Colonel picked a quarrel with the young guest, and challenged him to fight a duel at 4 o'clock next morning. Markham had no friends, so McDonald selected two very young Lieutenants, Lockhart and Pack, out of his own regiment as seconds; insisted upon two shots, and shot his guest through the body. There were circumstances of peculiar atrocity about this cold-blooded murder. The slight if not imaginary cause of offence, the fact of the challenger being the host of his victim and more than twenty years his senior; and the selection of mere boys of his own regiment as seconds, all added to the infamy of McDonald's conduct. The cowardly murderer ought to have been hanged. But he became General Sir John McDonald K.C.B.

David Markham went to Ireland to console his uncle and help him through the affair. This would appear to have been a role David Markham admirably fulfilled, as he would through his lifetime counsel family, friends, and his congregation through difficult times.

David Markham's ability to console would be sorely tested in December of 1833 when a major calamity struck the parish.

> The singers of the church, including the clerk, four other men, and several young girls had been singing the praises of their Saviour in Kelfield and the neighbouring townships. They were returning from Kelfield in a boat on the river Ouse in the evening of Thursday the 26th of December 1833 when the boat was upset by the tow rope of a barge, and every soul was drowned. The bodies were found one by one, washed up at different places during the succeeding days. The grief and consternation in the parish may be imagined. Families were left fatherless, others lost a dearly loved member, all were plunged in sorrow. There was need for comfort and support in this time of trouble and, in their vicar, the people of Stillingfleet had a friend who shared their feelings and was one of them…[4]

[4] Clements Markham goes on to note that in 1876, forty three years after the event, the Reverend W.A. Wightman, Vicar of Stillingfleet, stated that the villagers still talk of the accident and how it affected David Markham. Those that died were: William Bristow aged 55, Henry Spencer 44, Sarah Spencer 16, Elizabeth Spencer 14, Christopher Spencer 36, John Turner 55, Jane Turner 16, Elizabeth Buckle 15, Clarissa Sturdy 17, Thomas Webster 44, and Sarah Eccles 16.

Despite the heavy workload associated with his pastoral duties David continued to indulge his interest in history, and especially local history with which he was particularly interested. He continued to study and "...brought together a well selected library of chronicles and county histories, and of historical literature of later times, which was added to his fine editions of the classics and of English poets." He is described by his son Clements Markham as being a skilled draughtsman with a special talent for sketching architectural details.

In 1835, during a trip to Ireland where he visited Dublin, Belfast and Port Rush, he took the time to sketch the Round Tower of Clondelhim, the Giant's Causeway and Dunluce Castle, among other sites. He early on became interested in investigating the early history of the Markham family, and during visits to sites associated with the family would always take the time to sketch a tomb or the architectural details of a church. This practice would continue throughout his life, leaving a pictorial record in sketch and watercolour of both the areas in which he travelled and lived.

Like many antiquarians before him and after, his interests were not limited to one area of study. His interest in the history of the Markham family and Windsor College led him to study heraldry. He owned a fine collection of Roman and English coins, and is described as being particularly interested in the "new science" of geology.[5] He was particularly fascinated by molluscs, and had cabinets full of shells – of course all accurately named and annotated! His pastoral duties required a significant amount of travel and this facilitated his exploration of the region around York and the sites along the way to Windsor. He visited and made sketches of Rievaulx Abbey, the church at Kirby Wiske, Bolton and Kirkstall Abbeys, Ryder church, Flamborough, and the churches of Beverley, Conisborough and Riccall. He is described as having acquired a "profound knowledge" of ecclesiastical

[5] The 1830s was a period when geology was in its infancy. However this was rapidly changing due to the work of Lyell, and others. See, Stephen Baxter, *Revolutions in the Earth*. London: Weidenfeld & Nicolson, 2003

architecture and was on several occasions consulted during the restoration of York Minster.

With such broad interests it was only a matter of time before he would become actively involved in the archaeology of Yorkshire. In 1835 he gained his opportunity, taking part in an excavation with a Dr. Travis and Lord Feversham. They opened a Tumuli about 1.5 miles from Scarborough and 500 yards from the sea cliff.

> The Tumulus was 30 yards in circumference, and was found to contain an urn with ashes and calcined human bones, a stone hammer, and a flint spear head. They came to the conclusion that this was a secondary or subsequent deposit because it was nearer the surface than the apex of the covering stones of a *cistvaen* or rude stone coffin below. After much labour the interior was exposed to view, 3ft. 8 inches long by 1 ft. 8 inches. Into this narrow space the body of the personage had been thrust, with knees drawn to the breast, and a small vase on the left of the head. David Markham made accurate drawings to scale, of everything that was found...

His interests in archaeology would continue until his death in 1853, but his explorations would shift south from Yorkshire to Essex.

In 1838 he received news that he was soon to experience a change of circumstances. On March 2nd, 1838, he received the following letter from Earl de Grey:

> My Dear David,
>
> Some years ago I promised that when an opportunity arrived I would do myself the pleasure of putting a living into your hands. The one I then had in my eye, and which would have brought you to me as a neighbour is still full, by the vitality of a very old fellow; but a much better one has fallen to me by the death of the Bishop of Sodor and Man: viz Great Horkesley in Essex. It is worth nearly £900 per annum, a population of about 700 (all agriculturalists) a very good house, and about 56 miles from London and 6 from Colchester. It is not quite so near to Windsor as Clophill would have been, but the difference of income will pay the coach fare. I should have wished it to be nearer to Wrest but I could not, in justice to you, consult those wishes, when the benefit would be so

much better. Had they been more nearby alike in value, I own I should have been selfish enough to have waited.

I remain yours most truly

De Grey

Lady de Grey also wrote as follows:

My Dear David,

I cannot say the pleasure it gives me to be able to join most heartily with Lord de Grey in the offer of Great Horkesley; but you will excuse me if I tell you that if I had not the full conviction that you will be *quite* devoted to your parish, with all my regard for you, I should not have agreed to offering it to you.

I believe upon some points you and I do *not quite coincide* in our religious opinions, as I fancy I incline more to what are called evangelical; but I feel certain, dear David, that God's honor and glory will be your sole object, and that you will do your utmost to draw those we place under your charge to Christ as their only sure refuge. The patronage of livings is an awful responsibility, and it has not been without prayer and consideration that we have decided on making you this offer. I enclose you the Archbishop of York's answer to a confidential letter of enquiry on my part which I think will gratify you. As I am very desirous that lectures and reading to the poor should be encouraged at Great Horkesley, you will have to keep a Curate. I tell you all this, my dear David, as I think it my duty to lay my opinion of the duties of a Minister such as we wish to place at Great Horkesley.

Love to Kitty, most truly yours

H. de Grey

Leaving Stillingfleet would prove difficult as the Markhams had settled in and David had grown fond of his congregation. However, he felt that, "...as Rector of Great Horkesley, he would have a wider and more active sphere and greater opportunities of usefulness." The result was that on May 6th 1838 "...a farewell sermon was preached at Stillingfleet, the last sad leave takings were finished, and in June David Markham left his first cure, which he had held for twelve years, followed by the hearty good wishes and regrets of his parishioners."

CHAPTER ONE

THE MOVE TO HORKESLEY

After leaving Stillingfleet with his family in June 1838, David Markham was at Windsor during July, and in August went for a few weeks to Walton on the Naze, on the Essex coast, which was at a convenient distance from Great Horkesley. He here was much interested in the study of the Suffolk crag formation, and in making a collection of its tertiary fossils. The family was for a few days at the 'Three Cups' Hotel at Colchester, and was established in the Rectory at Great Horkesley by September 1838.

The Rectory is four miles north of Colchester, the straight road leading across a nearly flat country; and the houses and cottages of the parish being scattered along it. This road is called the 'Causeway' and probably the houses were gradually extended along it in the direction of Colchester, and away from the church as the land was enclosed. There is no connected village, and thus the church and rectory are removed from the inhabited part of the parish.

The Causeway leads direct from Colchester to the rectory lodge, and just before reaching it, the roads pass to the left and right, to Little Horkesley and Nayland. Here there is a plot of grass where, in the old days the Hadleigh coach, communicating with that from Colchester to London, used to take up and put down rectory passengers. From the lodge the drive to the rectory crosses a one acre park field with a row of ancient elms[6] leading to the churchyard, and then enters the pleasure ground. Thus the rectory, with the church near it and a small school house, stands away from the rest of the parish, on the verge, surrounded by its own glebe. The glebe is on the verge, too, of another region. All

[6] The author notes that all but seven of these oak trees were blown down in a storm in October of 1881.

towards Colchester is flat and uninteresting, but on the other side, at the end of the garden looking north, there is a beautiful view over the valley of the Stour, which separates Essex and Suffolk.[7] The river winds through rich meadows, and the hills rise with sufficient abruptness on either side to form a pleasing landscape, with the fields and well timbered hedge rows diversified by woods, and Flemish farm houses fronted by rows of stately willows.

Great Horkesley glebe is on the summit of the southern slope of the Stour valley. It consists of six fields surrounding the house and gardens, namely the Park-field to the south leading to the Causeway and the road to Colchester, three fields bordering on the road to Nayland and two facing to the west.

> * (Here there are five pages missing, part of which described the region and some of the walks that could be enjoyed.)

Another pleasant walk was through fields beyond the church yard, and up a lane to Little Horkesley where there is a little church containing most interesting monumental brasses, and an Italian villa-like house, with large portico, called Little Horkesley Hall. Even on the Essex side, the country is interesting, in the direction of Bergholt Heath, Pitchberry wood, and the Roman camp.

In 1838 the immediate neighbours were, in the parish, Mr. Stebbing Sadler, a gentleman farmer, at a place called Old House on the right of the Causeway going to Colchester; with a mother, a wife and five children; Major George Sadler; and old Dr. and Mrs. Harold at Horkesley Park. About three miles off was Westwood House built by Major Rooke, who had a wife and a family of handsome daughters. At Little Horkesley was Mr. Warren, the clergyman and squire, whose wife was a sister of Mrs Rooke. At Nayland lived the medical man, Dr. Edward Living, an agreeable neighbour with a large family; and the clergyman at Stoke, also with a large family, was Mr. Torlesse, an active and studious man, and a Hebrew scholar. At Tendring was Sir Joshua Bowley, a rough

[7] Here the author, in a brief anecdote in the margins, notes that the region was home and inspiration to two of Britain's most famous painters, Gainsborough and Constable.

old Admiral with no family, but an amiable and pleasant wife. The Rector of Wiston was the Reverend Charles Birch, son of the Dean of Battle, whose wife was a Miss Burnett of Aberdeen.[8] They had two daughters, Nelly and Maggy, the youngest born in 1839. These were the only near neighbours who were really sympathetic, and became attached friends. At Colchester was the Reverend James Round; and afterwards the Reverend J. Papillon,[9] Rector of Lexden, and the Reverend Louis Owen[10] of Trinity Church in Colchester, with their families, formed intimacies at Horkesley Rectory which ripened into close friendship. Mr. Strong, the Rector of Myland, a parish which intervenes between Horkesley and Colchester, and Dr. and Mrs Harold[11] of Horkesley Park were also on terms of intimate friendship at the rectory; as well as Mr. Torlesse, the Vicar of Stoke.[12]

---

[8] Author's note: Birch was of St. John's College, Oxford, where he received a B.A. in 1829. He was born in 1806 and Rector of Wiston since 1832.

[9] Author's note: He died at a great age in October 1889.

[10] Author's note: The Owens lived in St. Mary's Terrace on the Lexden Road, where he had pupils: Mr. Biddulph, sons of Bishop Wilberforce, of Duke of Argyll, of Sir Stafford Northcote. He was a short time afterwards, at Wadingham in Lincolnshire, then Rector of Wouston in Hampshire, from 1870. He died at Wouston on January 7th 1884.

[11] Author's note: Dr. Harold practiced at Nayland and, having made a fortune, retired to Horkesley Park. He married first Isabella Harriet Living who died on February 23rd 1798, and who was buried at Wiston. Her nephew was Dr. Living, who succeeded Dr. Harold in the practice at Nayland. Dr. Harold's second wife was Miss Whitmore, daughter of the miller at Wiston Mill. Dr. Harold and his second wife were also buried at Wiston.

[12] Author's note: Reverend Charles Martin Torlesse became Vicar of Stoke in 1832. He married Catharine Gurney Wakefield (born April 26 1793) who died in 1873. They had nine children: 1. Charles born 2nd May 1825. An engineer in Canterbury New Zealand where he married and had a son and three daughters. He came home and died on 14th November 1868 and was buried at Stoke. His son Arthur is a sub Lieutenant. 2. Reverend Henry, born 1833. He died in New Zealand on December 17th 1870. He married there, and had eight children. One son, Henry, was in the navy. 3. Priscilla. 4. Anna Maria, born in 1826, died 1838. 5. Catharine, born in 1835, died in 1852. 6. Susan, born in 1831, married in February 1860 to Dr. Bridges. Died 7th December 1860. 7. Emily, married Reverend C. Holland. 8. Fanny. Old Mr. Torlesse died in July 1881, having been Vicar of Stoke for 49 years. Succeeded by Mr. Hodges, previously the Curate. Then Mr. Wilkinson, an accomplished mechanician who, the author notes, was in possession of the skull of the Lord Protector Oliver.

CHAPTER TWO

THE HISTORY OF GREAT AND LITTLE HORKESLEY

The parishes of Great and Little Horkesley were formerly part and parcel of the manor of Nayland in the valley of the Stour. Morant derives the name from *Horseley* (horse pasture); but David Markham suggested a more probable derivation from the British word *Hor,* a boundary, *Caes* a camp, and *Ley*, meadows: hence *Horcaesley*, or "the fields about the boundary camp," which he placed either upon what is now called Horkesley Hill, overlooking Suffolk – the country of the Iceni,[13] or at the site of Pitchberry wood.[14]

The name does not occur in Domesday because it was then included in Nayland, but the two Horkesley parishes appear to have been separated before the reign of John.[15] To an antiquary Little Horkesley is much the most interesting of the two. From it a knightly family took its name, which flourished during the 13th and 14th centuries. There are three wooden effigies in the

---

[13] The Iceni were a Celtic people that occupied Norfolk and North-west Suffolk at the time of the Roman invasion. Initially friendly with Rome, relations soured in A.D. 47 when the Governor Ostorius Scapula attempted to disarm them. Rebellion followed, and would be repeated in A.D. 60 with the outbreak of the much more serious Boudican rebellion which threatened Roman control. See, Peter Salway, *Roman Britain.* (Oxford: Oxford University Press, 1981) pp.44, 90, 100-123. Also see, John Waite, *Boudica's Last Stand.* Stroud: The History Press, 2007; and Guy De La Bedoyere, *Defying Rome.* Stroud: Tempus, 2003.

[14] The Rev. Henry Jenkins, writing in 1841, described Pitchbury as an earthwork that was oval in shape and of about 6 acres. *Victoria Histories Of the Counties of England: Essex.* Vol. 1. Reprint, (Folkestone, Kent: William Dawson and Sons Ltd., 1977) p.285

[15] King John reigned from 1199-1216.

church, two of crusaders and one of a female, which are probably memorials of the Horkesleys.

In about 1375, the Horkesleys having become extinct, the manor of Little Horkesley became the property of Robert de Swinborne. It remained in possession of his descendants for nearly three centuries, passing through Swinbornes to Berners, Fynderne, and Wentworth. Sir Robert Swinborne, who died in 1391, and his son Sir Thomas, were buried in the chancel. The latter was Mayor of Bordeaux and Constable of Frousac in Guienne. On an altar tomb are two very beautiful brass effigies of father and son side by side.

The Wentworths, descended from the Swinbornes, suffered in the civil war, and in 1660 Little Horkesley Manor was sold to Azariah Husbands, whose son Edward built a commodious brick house there, which was replaced by Mr. Warren's Italian Villa. The grandson, the Reverend James Husbands, Vicar of the parish and of Fordham, died childless in 1750 and was succeeded by his niece Anne the wife of Dr. William Blair Warren of Little Horkesley, Vicar 1826-1856.

At Westwood, in the same parish, a family named Lynne was established from 1616 to the end of the last century; but in 1838 it belonged to the Rookes.[16]

The Priory of Little Horkesley was founded, in the time of Henry I,[17] by Robert son of Godebold, for Cluniac Monks to be provided from the larger monastery of Thetford. Wiston church was assigned to the Priory, and it was the duty of the Monks to

[16] Author's note: Major Charles Rooke married Emily, daughter of General Watson of Westwood, sister of Mrs. Blair Warren. They had two sons, George and Frederick, and four daughters. The eldest, Julia, married Mr. Humphreys (died in 1837 aged 28) and afterwards to her cousin Mr. Rooke. The second married Mr. Harrenne, the third married the Reverend Markham Mills in 1842 and the youngest – Elvira – never married. Mrs. Rooke died 28th July 1854, aged 60. The Rookes were ruined, and sold Westwood to Mr. Leveson Gower, who sold it to Mr. MacAndrew, a wealthy merchant, who became a widow with a family. In 1876 he married Helen, daughter of the Reverend Charles Birch, Rector of Wiston, and widow of Mr. Gataher. The author notes here that Westwood was 109 acres and worth £311.

[17] Henry I, the youngest son of William the Conqueror, reigned from 1100-1135.

serve the churches of Little Horkesley and Wiston. The Priory stood to the north of the church. It was one of the small monasteries which Wolsey, in 1525, got leave from the Pope to make part of the endowment of his college at Oxford, and upon the Cardinal's fall it escheated to the crown.[18] Soon afterwards the priory buildings appear to have been pulled down, including the church, for the present edifice, consisting of a nave, chancel, and south aisle, is late perpendicular, though it contains most interesting monuments of a much earlier date.

In 1623 the rectory and church were granted to Sir Humphrey Winch[19] and, passing with the manor, they became the property of the Husbands, and through them of Mr. Blair Warren. The site of the priory, with a farm passed through several hands, and in the last century James Joscelyn built a house on it.

Great Horkesley is a much larger parish, consisting of 3084 acres, of which 2592 are arable, 258 pasture and 134 wood. It is bounded on the north by the river Stour which separates it from Suffolk, on the east by the parish of Boxted, on the south by Nyland and West Bergholt, and on the west by Bergholt and Little Horkesley. It is about four miles long from the Stour to the top of

[18] Cardinal Thomas Wolsey (1470/71-1530) began his meteoric rise to prominence under Henry VII, but is best known for the part he would play as Henry VIII's most influential advisor. By the early 1520s he had established himself as the second most powerful individual in the Kingdom and had enormous influence. During the 1520s Wolsey closed down a number of monastic communities that were struggling, setting a precedent for the Dissolution of the Monasteries that would follow (1536-1540) under Cromwell. Wolsey is best remembered for his failure to resolve the "King's Great Matter" and procure Henry's sought after divorce from Catherine of Aragon so that he could marry Anne Boleyn. See, Sybil M. Jack, "Wolsey, Thomas (1470/71-1530)" *Oxford Dictionary of National Biography*. (Oxford: Oxford University Press, 2004) Online Ed. Also see, John Guy, *Tudor England*. (Oxford: Oxford University Press, 1988) pp.80-153.

[19] Sir Humphrey Winch (1554/5-1625) a judge called to the bench in 1595. He spent time as part of the Irish administration in Dublin, and in 1604, under the newly crowned King James VI and I, addressed parliament on church reform, privileges and Catholic recusants. Wilfrid Prest, "Winch, Sir Humphrey (1554/5-1625) *Oxford Dictionary of National Biography*. (Oxford: Oxford University Press, 2004) Online Ed.

the hill beyond Black Brook, and averages about two and a half miles in width.

In 1256 the Manor of Great Horkesley was granted to John de Burgh, who had free warren there. It next came into the family of the Lords Scrope of Masham, and remained with them until 1515. But in 1540 it appears to have been in the crown, for Henry VIII granted it to William Shelley,[20] a descendant of the Scropes, in whose family it remained until the end of that century. In the reign of James I[21] it was sold to Paul Bayning, father of the First Lord Bayning, who took the title of his barony from this place. On September 24th 1612 he was created a Baronet, and on the 27th of February 1628, Baron Bayning of Horkesley. His daughter Anne brought the manor to Aubrey de Vere, the last Earl of Oxford,[22] whose heir sold it to a rich clothier at Dedham named Freeman. His heirs enjoyed it until 1838, when it was sold to a man named Cuddon. The manor house stands to the east of the Causeway, near the southern extremity of the parish.

The estate of Horkesley Park, on the slope overlooking Nayland, formed part of the manorial demesne of the Scropes, but when Thomas Lord Scrope[23] died, in 1492, without male issue,

---

[20] Author's note: Parish Register contains the following entry: "William Shelley Esq., Lord of this town of Much Horkesley: buried April 24th 1597."

[21] James the VI of Scotland became James I of England in 1603 with the Union of the Crowns and reigned until his death in 1624.

[22] Aubrey de Vere was an opportunistic figure with a close association with Essex. Born in 1627, he would remain a somewhat shadowy figure until the Restoration, where he was nominated to be one of six peers to invite Charles II back to England. He became Lord Lieutenant of Essex in 1660, and held the post until his death in 1703. He enjoyed the favouritism of Charles II, being rewarded with a variety of posts, including that of High Steward of Colchester. Despite the good fortune he acquired by his close relationship with Charles II, he was quick to change sides and prosper under William III. See, Victor Stater, "Vere, Aubrey de, Twentieth Earl of Oxford (1627-1703) *Oxford Dictionary of National Biography.* (Oxford: Oxford University Press, 2004) Online Ed.

[23] The author is possibly referring to Thomas Scrope, bishop of Dromore, who died in 1492, however it is possible that he is referring to another member of the Scrope family that were landowners in Leicestershire. Thomas Scrope was a Carmelite monk who wrote several works on the Carmelites and, in 1450, was appointed bishop of Dromore in Ireland. He however spent most of his time in the Diocese of Norwich, where he is reputed to have walked barefoot through

his estates vested in his three daughters, and Horkesley came to Margery the wife of Sir Christopher Danby. Their grandson sold it to Jerome Weston, whose grandson the Earl of Portland sold it, in 1639, to William Gibbs, one of whose descendants parted with it to the Rowleys of Tendring. The estate still belongs to Tendring with the exception of the house and 40 acres of land, which were sold to Samuel Gibbs, whose son sold it to Dr. Harrold, a retired medical man; from whom Horkesley Park was purchased, in 1842, by Captain Kelso (formerly of the 72nd).

Another estate in the parish of Great Horkesley is that of Brewood Hall which belonged to John Lucas the Town Clerk of Colchester in the time of Edward VI. It descended from him to his great grandson Sir Charles Lucas,[24] who was condemned to be shot, after the siege of Colchester in 1648, for having broken his parole of honor to Lord Fairfax, not again to serve against the Parliament. He died childless, and Brewood Hall passed to his eldest brother Lord Lucas, and through his daughter to the Earls of Kent, and their descendant Earl de Grey. In 1838 the tenant of Brewood Hall was Mr. Partridge, a farmer and the Rector's Churchwarden. The family of Sadler has possessed freehold property in the parish for upwards of a century. Woodhouse, an ancient moated place, now a farm house, was bought by Lord Ashburton;[25] and Messrs. Fisher Hobbs, Keningale, Knoff, and

---

the countryside preaching to all that would listen. At his death in 1492 he was said to be nearly 100 years of age. Richard Copsey, "Scrope, Thomas (d.1492)" *Oxford Dictionary of National Biography*. (Oxford: Oxford University Press, 2004) Online Ed.

[24] Sir Charles Lucas (1612/13-1648), a cavalry officer for the Royalist cause during the civil war, was executed following the surrender of Colchester in 1648. He is described as being, next to Charles I, "the pre-eminent royalist martyr of the civil wars". Barbara Donagan, "Lucas, Sir Charles (1612/13-1648) *Oxford Dictionary of National Biography*, (Oxford: Oxford University Press, 2004) Online Ed.

[25] Alexander Baring, first Baron Ashburton (1773-1848). Baring was a prominent merchant and Banker with commercial interests in the United States. He is perhaps best known for his negotiations in the Louisiana Purchase in 1803. Baring entered politics in 1806 and was elevated to the House of Lords in 1835. Over his career he amassed a vast fortune and invested heavily in property. John Orbell, "Baring, Alexander, first Baron Ashburton (1773-1848)" *Oxford*

Haywood were farmers who, in 1838, held freehold estates in Great Horkesley.

To the north west of Woodhouse, and between Pitchberry Wood and Bergholt Heath, is an ancient entrenched camp containing 9 acres. It is of oval form and protected by a double fosse and vallum,[26] the principal entrances to it lying north and south. It is situated exactly on the line of Roman road between Camalodunum (Colchester)[27] and Wormingford. In the year 1840 the whole encampment was very perfect, and that part of it which extends into the wood was not injured. But the then occupier, hoping to derive benefit by levelling the fosse and vallum, has in a great measure destroyed the outlines of the camp, without deriving a corresponding profit.

It has been a question whether this camp is Roman or not. It was probably originally a British *Oppidum*,[28] afterwards made use of by the Romans and adapted to their habits, though retaining the form in which it was found. It is generally called the "Rampart Field."

In times previous to the Reformation Great Horkesley appears to have been a very populous place, for an agricultural parish. At the suppression of chantries it was said "The town of Much Horkesley ys a very great and populous towne, and the moste parts thereof is upland, having in it the number of 200 houselyng people." In 1811 the population was 571, it was 623 in 1821, in 1831 it was

---

Dictionary of National Biography. (Oxford: Oxford University Press, 2004) Online Ed.

[26] A *Vallum* is "a palisaded bank or rampart, formed of earth dug up from the ditch or Fosse around a Roman military camp. Lesley Brown (Ed.), *The New Shorter Oxford English Dictionary.* Vol. 2. (Oxford: Clarendon Press, 1993) p.3542.

[27] Colchester was established as an important Roman centre immediately following the invasion of 43 A.D. Recent excavations have shown that a legionary fortress had been established, but that this had later been dismantled as the town grew in importance. Roman Colchester included a Temple to the Emperor Claudius, a theatre, bath-house, a circus and a range of civic buildings. At its height it was a densely packed urban centre, home to legionary veterans and natives alike. For more on Roman Colchester see, John Wacher, *The Towns of Roman Britain.* 2nd Ed. (London: B.T. Batsford, 1995) pp.113-132.

[28] A fortified town. Lesley Brown (Ed.), *The New Shorter Oxford English Dictionary.* Vol. 2. (Oxford: Clarendon Press, 1993) p.208.

697, in 1841 it was 730, and in 1851 it was 747. In 1851 there were 164 inhabited houses; and of the 164 families, 132 were occupied in agriculture, 29 in trade. There were 12 farmers employing labourers, and 8 farms held by non-residents. The 747 souls included 372 males and 375 females. In 1861 the population was 769, it was 844 in 1871, and 794 (a decrease) in 1881: houses 188, 1891-783, and 180 houses.

The Rectory belonged to the Cluniac Priory of Prittlewell in Essex, founded in the reign of Henry II; and the patronage continued with that religious house until the reformation. On April 9th 1545 Henry VIII granted it to John de Vere, Earl of Oxford,[29] who sold it to John Lucas, the Town Clerk of Colchester. He presented to it in 1559, and it has continued in his posterity ever since. Earl de Grey, in 1838, was the representation of the Lucas family.

The church of Great Horkesley is not interesting. It is built of rubble and plastered, with stone quorins and dressings; and consists of a nave and chancel, north aisle and chantry, and tower, all in the latest perpendicular style.[30] There is nothing older except

[29] The author is referring to John de Vere, the 16th Earl of Oxford (1516-1562), The 15th Earl of Oxford had been a favourite of Henry VIII, serving with him in France in 1513 at the Battle of the Spurs, supporting Henry's bid to Marry Anne Boleyn, and then speaking out against her in 1536 when it was alleged that she had taken a string of lovers. He was reputedly granted monastic lands in Essex worth £160 per annum during the Dissolution, lands that may well have included the Cluniac Priory of Prittlewell mentioned by the author as being granted in 1545. The 16th Earl similarly enjoyed Henry's favour, accompanying him on his Boulogne campaign in 1544. The 16th Earl appears to have been a rather nefarious figure with numerous mistresses and whom kept company with many unsavoury figures. See, Jonathan Hughes, "Vere, John de, sixteenth Earl of Oxford (1516-1562)" *Oxford Dictionary of National Biography*. (Oxford: Oxford University Press, 2004) Online Ed.

[30] The perpendicular style of architecture has been described as the "last great culminating phase of Gothic architecture in England." It is identified by the vertical lines of its window tracery, the complexity of decoration and sheer size of windows to allow greater light to flood the interior. Many parish churches constructed in the 14th and 15th centuries, especially in East Anglia, adopted this style and remain as excellent examples. The Royal Chapel of St. George at Windsor, with which David Markham had an intimate familiarity, is another excellent example. John Cannon (Ed.), *The Oxford Companion to British History*. (Oxford: Oxford University Press, 2002) pp.742-43.

the tomb stone of the earliest recorded rector in the chancel, with a cross, and the date 1326 "Richard Oliver." In 1838 there were high square pews, painted deal alter rails, mean deal reading desk and pulpit, and a hideous deal gallery across the west end of the church, put up in 1821.

> The first recorded Rector was Richard Oliver, who died in 1326. The first Protestant was Robert Coates, presented by John Lucas in 1559. He was deprived in 1562. In 1683 the Earl of Kent presented for the first time to Reverend Robert Harrison, who was followed in 1732 by the Reverend John Morse. In 1756 the Reverend Dr. John Browne became Rector and continued here until 1771. He was the author of *Estimate of the Manners and Principles of the Times*, a work which excited uncommon attention at the time it was published, and went rapidly through many editions. He also wrote a *Dissertation on Poetry and Music*, and various other works. Dr. Browne was followed by Dr. John Cock, who was Rector from 1771 to 1796, as well as Vicar of Dedham and Incumbent of Thaxted. He is said to have been a very eccentric character. His successor was the Reverend Philip Yorke, Prebendary of Ely, who built the rectory house. On the death of Mr. Yorke, in 1817, Dr. William Ward, the Bishop of Sodor and Man, resigned the living of Nyland for that of Great Horkesley.[31] He was presented by Amabel, Countess de Grey in her own right. After his death on January 26th 1838, Earl de Grey, on the 26th of March 1838, presented the living of Great Horkesley to the Reverend David Markham.

[31] Author's note: Dr. William Ward, born in 1761, was Rector of Great Horkesley from 1817 to 1838. He was a kindly Irishman and tutor to Thomas Philip Frederick John Robinson, sons of Lord Grantham, the former afterwards Earl de Grey, the latter 'Prosperity' Robinson, Chancellor of the Exchequer and Earl of Ripon. Dr. Ward married Ann, daughter of Mr. Hammersley, a banker. He died on January 26th 1838, and was buried on the N.W. end of the churchyard. In the same grave was buried Mrs. Ward who died April 1st 1841, aged 67. Their children were: Thomas William, born in 1810, died at Cambridge aged 19; Charlotte born in 1806, married D.B. Chapman Esq., and died on September 3rd 1828; Mary Caroline born 1808, died in 1844 aged 35; Amabel Catherine born in 1815, and died in 1817 aged 2; Reverend William Ward; and Caroline, died aged 83.

Chapter Three

IMPROVEMENTS AT HORKESLEY, NEW DUTIES, LOSSES AND ILLNESSES, JOURNEYS AND OCCUPATIONS 1839-1841

Great Horkesley was a place of exile from friends and kindred. But, although it was a banishment, the change opened a wider field of usefulness and entailed heavier and more extensive duties and responsibilities. During the autumn of 1838 the family was settling into the new home. The rectory house and glebe had great capabilities, but nearly everything had to be done. It was necessary at once to build a kitchen with servant's rooms above, and this was completed while the family was at Walton. The library, on the left of the hall, was a cheerful room and contained three large bookcases holding the historical and general literature and the cabinet of coins. To the right the study held two large bookcases containing works on theology and divinity; while the closet beyond, opening to the backyard, was converted into a dispensary and surgery. The hall was not so large as that of Stillingfleet, or so well adapted for receiving the collection of shells and fossils, which were not all unpacked and arranged for some years.

The necessary improvements were also commenced in the grounds, the walk round the glebe was attended to, and peeps were cut to bring in view the church towers, and other picturesque bits. In 1840 a small flower garden was made in front of the west side of the house, with a hedge of *Pyrus Japonica*, an arcade for roses and a very pretty summer house was built, the drive was altered, and the outer flower garden was much enlarged, several large trees being enclosed, which formerly stood outside. A sunk fence was also filled up.

The school and master's house were built in 1816 by Mr. Yorke, on a small piece of land adjoining the north side of the churchyard, which was leased to the Rector for the time being for 99 years at a minimal rent, by Mr. Peter Coveney. The building was erected by subscription, but it is ill built, inconvenient, and ill contrived. In 1828 the Bishop of Sodor and Man leased an additional piece of ground as a garden and play ground for £5.0.0 a year. As there was no school at Little Horkesley, the children from that parish also attended. In 1841 Mr. Markham, at his own expense, improved the schoolroom and extended it 6 feet in length. The master and mistress, who were found there in 1838, George Howlett and his wife, were proved to be incompetent. They were dismissed in 1844, and Mr. And Mrs. Salmon took their places. The number of children averaged from 110 to 120.

More regularity was also introduced into the services of the church. The Holy Communion, which had hitherto been administered irregularly and not more than six times in the year was, in 1838, arranged to be administered eight times and at fixed periods. The baptisms were celebrated during divine service from 1838, the clothing and shoe clubs were placed on a thoroughly efficient footing, and a lending library was established. The Curate, in 1838, was the Reverend James Crebbin who had been there since 1833, succeeding Sir Augustus Hennisher Bart., who was Curate from 1829 to 1833. Mr. Crebbin was replaced, in July 1840, by the Reverend Charles Holland (born 25 August 1817).

On the 15th of December 1838 David Markham's fifth child was born at Great Horkesley, a daughter named Georgina Elizabeth. Her godfather was Henry Clements Esq. M.P. of Ashfield Co. Cavan, and her godmothers Mrs. Baillie (afterwards Countess of Haddington) and Miss Georgina Milner.

In the year 1839 David Markham undertook the wardship of two of his wife's cousins, John and Henry Clements, which then and afterwards entailed upon him much harassing trouble and responsibility. But this was foreseen and cheerfully entered upon. John was then aged thirteen, and Henry ten. They had been left orphans, their father dying in 1836 and their mother in 1839, and they found a kind welcome and a second home at Horkesley.[32]

In 1839, too, David Markham sent his two sons to school – first to a Private school at Cheam, in Surrey, under the Reverend W. Browne; preparatory to Westminster. The coach – the 'Wellington' – still ran from Colchester to Grace church street (the Spread Eagle) and the boys went on by the Brixton coach, from *Belle Sauvage* in Ludgate Hill, to Cheam.

On the 9th of May 1839 David Markham performed the service at the marriage of his cousin Lady Seymour, youngest daughter of his aunt Lady Mansfield, to Colonel Francis Seymour,[33] eldest son of Rear Admiral Sir George Seymour, which took place from Langham House.[34]

Two of the Canons of Windsor died in 1840, Dr. Goodall the old Provost of Eton,[35] and Dr. the Honourable Jacob Marsham. Lord Wriathesley Russell was appointed in the room of the former. David Markham succeeded to the house of Dr. Marsham, the charm of which was that nearly every room had windows looking out over the glorious view with the Thames winding through its meadows, and the Brocas clump, Clewer church spire, and the

---

[32] Author's note: The boys had been at a school kept by a Mr. Thompson at Sheen. John, as it had been the wish of his parents, went to Eton for a short time, then to a Private Tutor, Mr. Hume at Me on Stoke in Hampshire, then to a Tutor in Belgium, and then into a cavalry regiment. Henry went to a school at Nockholt under Mr. Sutcliffe, then to Rugby, and eventually to Christ Church, Oxford, after which he attended holy orders.

[33] Francis George Hugh Seymour (1812-1884) was the eldest son of Sir George Francis Seymour, a prominent naval officer who rose to the rank of Vice-Admiral and Lord of the Admiralty. Francis served as Lord Chamberlain from 1874 to 1879. J.K. Laughton, "Seymour, Sir George Francis (1787-1870)" *Oxford Dictionary of National Biography*. (Oxford: Oxford University Press, 2004) Online Ed.

[34] Author's note: Colonel and lady Emily Seymour succeeded, in 1870, as Marquis and Marchioness of Hertford. At their marriage they presented David Markham with an escritoire table of the time of Louis XV.

[35] Joseph Goodall (1760-1840) was appointed Headmaster of Eton in 1801. In 1808 he became a canon at Windsor, and in 1809 became Provost of Eton at the request of George III. Leslie Stephen, "Goodall, Joseph (1760-1840)" *Oxford Dictionary of National Biography*. (Oxford: Oxford University Press, 2004) Online Ed.

distant Buckinghamshire hills beyond. On the inner side the house looked upon the north transept of St. George's chapel; and here the façade was of brick, with pilasters attributed to Inigo Jones.[36] The outer side formed the outer wall of the castle, the dining room, with the schoolroom above it and the boys' bed room above that, having a bow with three windows. And the rest of the house consisting of the drawing rooms and a study en suite with windows on either side, and bed rooms above, besides other bed rooms in odd nooks and crannies. For these cloister houses are full of long passages with many turnings, and stairs up and down, leading to rooms in most unexpected corners, and to doors opening on unsuspected leads and roofs. Mr. Markham knocked another window through the thickness of the castle wall, in the back drawing room, which not only afforded another view; but formed a charming recess for drawing or writing in, the walls being eight feet thick. In this year, too, he took the Canon's Slopes in hand. Below the north terrace of the castle apportion of the steep and precipitous slope covered with trees, and a few acres below, outside the houses of the Naval Knights, belonged to the Dean and Chapter. Hitherto it had been a wilderness overgrown with nettles, and covered with refuse heaps. David Markham drew out plans, and converted it into a most pleasant garden and lawn, with well kept gravel walks up the steep slopes, a summer house, and monuments where, as Fox records, three lay clerks of St. Georges' Chapel were burnt to death in the days of Queen Mary.

All the children having had the whooping cough in the summer of 1840 at Windsor, the family went to Ramsgate for a month in the autumn, sleeping at the 'Adelaide Hotel' near

[36] Inigo Jones was an influential architect during the reigns of James I and Charles I. He began designing stage sets and costumes for the court of James I, rose to the position of Surveyor General. Inigo Jones was heavily influenced by classical design and is attributed with breaking with medieval and Elizabethan traditions and introducing Renaissance designs into England. His greatest achievements include: the Banqueting House at Whitehall, The Queen's House at Greenwich and the Piazza at Covent Garden. For a complete study of the importance of Inigo Jones see, Michael Leapman, *Inigo*. (London: Headline Books, 2004).

London Bridge and going down the river in a steamer. While at Ramsgate Mr. Markham took his two boys across to Boulogne, the first time of being abroad, where they spent a delightful week in the midst of all the fetes consequent on the inauguration of Napoleon's statue. It was then that they went to the theatre for their first time, and saw some of Dejazets' inimitable acting. Their father afterwards took them to see Macready[37] in Lytton Bulwer's 'Money' at the Haymarket.[38]

David Markham's great happiness was to witness and join in the pleasures of children. In the winter of 1839 he organized some charades for his children and those of the neighbourhood; the acting being in the dining room; where the stage arrangements were very complete. There were two words 'Prison' and 'Catastrophe'. The word 'son' was represented by Shakespeare's scene in Henry IV, of Prince Henry putting on the old king's crown; the two parts being taken by David and Clements. 'Prison' was the murder of Prince Arthur. The part of Arthur was taken by his daughter Selina; and he himself cut out and made the little blue coat trimmed with fur, and the cap; arranged everything, and drilled and rehearsed the actors in their parts.

---

[37] William Charles Macready (1793-1873) was a prominent actor from a family long familiar with the stage. From a very early age William showed great promise and would go on to make his first appearance on the stage at age seventeen. By 1840, when David Markham attended one of his plays, Macready had established himself as one of the foremost actors of his day and had also experimented as a theatre manager. He was instrumental in encouraging the production of new plays, which brought him into contact with many of the leading literary figures of his day, including: Lytton Bulwer, Carlyle, Tennyson, Dickens, Thackeray and others. See, Richard Foulkes, "Macready, William Charles (1793-1873)" *Oxford Dictionary of National Biography*. (Oxford: Oxford University Press, 2004) Online Ed.

[38] Edward George Lytton Bulwer (1803-1873) was a prominent writer and politician. He published his first work, Ismael: an Oriental Tale, in 1820 and by the 1830s had become one of the countries most popular writers. He wrote five plays for William Macready between 1836 and 1840, his comedy *Money* (1840) being one of his most successful plays. Andrew Brown, "Lytton, Edward George Earle Lytton Bulwer, first Baron Lytton (1803-1873)" *Oxford Dictionary of National Biography*. (Oxford: Oxford University press, 2004) Online Ed.

At Christmas 1840 there were charades at Horkesley on a still grander scale, with a regular stage and foot and side lights, before a very large audience. David Markham again cut out and made all the principal dresses, arranged the parts, and superintended the rehearsing and grouping. The words were 'Courtesy' and 'Dynasty'. 'Court' was a trial, 'Easy' was Columbus and the egg, 'Courtesy' – Sir Walter Raleigh throwing his cloak down before the Queen. Elizabeth was a very pretty Miss Living in superb attire. 'Die'was Cardinal Wolsey arriving at Leicester, acted by David, the hat and robes being made by his father. 'Nasty' was Mrs. Squeers feeding the boys, an uproarious scene in which all the smaller children could join. 'Dynasty' was the landing of Charles II at Dover, received by Monk; another grand display or gorgeous costumes.

At Horkesley David Markham enjoyed long visits from his mother. She came with her own carriage, her maid Shipley, and her man Beveridge, an old soldier of the 72nd who had been her son Warren's servant at the Cape. Latterly she had lived almost entirely at Horkesley, and was there all the winter of 1840-41. She died very suddenly of heart disease at Horkesley, on the 25th of March 1841, and was buried at the west end of the churchyard under a stone slab. Her son also placed a cross plate on a black marble slab, with an inscription to her memory, on the north wall of the chancel. 1841 was indeed a year of great anxiety as well as of sorrow. Mrs. Markham was most dangerously ill, and was only saved through the constant watching and care of her husband and of Dr. Living; and the little girl Gena was so very delicate that it was scarcely hoped that she would live. For a year she was kept in one room with an equal temperature; and her Father exercised his wonderful ingenuity to amuse her. Among other things he cut out, sewed, and set up a complete Red Indian's tent in miniature, with paintings round it, taken from Catlin. At this time also he started a printing press in his study, as he had found it useful to have the means of printing notices for the clubs. His second son had written a childish History of England and , in September 1841, he printed, without any aid, a complete edition of it as a bit of practice in printing, with stiff cover, title, paged and stitched; as the first book issued from the "Tyro Press of Great Horkesley."

In the same autumn he went, with his two boys, on two pleasant trips into Suffolk, chiefly with architectural objects. Starting early in the morning they drove, through Nayland and Stoke, and Boxford, to Lavenham where they stopped to examine the church. They then went on to Bury St. Edmunds, and passed the rest of the day in seeing the Norman tower and the different churches, putting up at the "Angel Inn", and returning next day. The second trip was to Colchester, and thence, by coach (the Star) to Ipswich; where the afternnon was passed in seeing the curious old houses with their oak carving, the churches, and the shipping. Next day they went down the Orwell in the steamer "Orion" to Harwich, and went across the harbour in a boat to see Landguard Fort and its fine fig trees. David Markham also paid a visit to Captain May, a rough old sailor who had been master of the Packet in which he and his brother William had gone from Harwich to Gottenburg, eighteen years before. They slept at Harwich, and went home next day.

In April 1841, Lieutenant Colonel Charles Markham of the 60th Rifles, who had been stationed for some time at Corfu, paid his last visit to his brother David at Horkesley. He was then in very bad health. He went to Jamaica in command of his regiment, and died there on April 22nd 1842, leaving an only child, a boy named Charles who became the ward of his uncle William at Becca.

In the winter of 1841 David Markham was in Yorkshire, paying visits at Esholt, Becca, and Nunappleton. He also went over to Stillingfleet, for the first time since his resignation, and saw all the people there and at Kelfield, who greeted him with unfeigned delight. His arm was quite tired with the incessant shaking, and his second visit and parting caused almost as great a pang as the farewell three years before.

~ David W. C. Markham ~

Born Dec 25th 1828
Died May 17th 1850

Mr Masters was succeeded as Steward at Nunappleton, in 1854, by Mr Giddy; and he was followed in 1858 by Mr Wright. Mr Masters died in 1870.

Mr Forbes (Agent)

Mr Mac Bean (Agent) 1885.–

~ Mr Masters ~
(Steward at Nunappleton)

~ William Randolph ~
David's friend and schoolfellow –

Mrs Egerton

Mary and Lucy Egerton

Margaret Birch

Mrs George Milner

Born Jan 24th 1793.
Married Sept 4th 1816.
Widow 1824.
Died Dec 9th 1878.

~ Lady and Miss Duncan ~

George Egerton
Born Nov 2d 1837
Married Aug 5th 1865

Frederick W. Egerton

Richard V. Hamilton R.N.

~ James Graham Goodenough ~

Born Dec 3rd 1830.
Naval Cadet May 7th 1844.
Lieut. June 23rd 1851.
Comm. Feb 26th 1858.
Captain May 9th 1863.
Married May 30th 1864.
Commodore May 22nd 1873 (Australia)
Died Aug 20th 1875

~ Mrs Strickland ~
(Gena Milner)

Born — April 1st 1816.
Married — Feb 19th 1850.
Died — June 16th 1864.

Willy Wickham

Born July 10th 1831.
Called to the Bar 1857.
married May 9th 1860

~ Georgie and Cicely Neville ~

* Seymour Neville was also Vicar of Wraysbury near Windsor. In 1869 he gave up the Windsor Canonry and Wraysbury, and became Rector of Ockham in Surrey. He married Agnes daughter of Mr Rooby, (Canon of Windsor) in 1859, but she died in 1860. Her sister, Miss Rooby afterwards kept house for him. He retired from Ockham, and died at Butleigh Court, aged 82, Dec 14th 1905.

Rear Admiral Sir George F. Seymour G.C.H.-C.B ~

~ Mr & Mrs Crompton Stansfield ~

~ Laura Markham (Mrs Muir) ~

Born March 14th 1804
Married Feb 7th 1825
Died March 9th 1878.

Clements R. Markham

Albert H. Markham   Clements R. Markham

George S. Owen

(Taken at Penzance)

~ Henry Milner ~

Born Dec 19th 1823.
Died – June 9th 1876.

Constance Carden

~ Archdeacon Bentinck ~

Born 1784
Married 1814
Died 1868

Selina Markham.

~ Lieut. Albert H. Markham ~
R.N.

~ Emma Stansfield ~

CHAPTER FOUR

PURCHASE OF A HOUSE FOR THE CURATE, RESTORATIONS AT ST. GEORGE'S CHAPEL, SOCIETY AT HORKESLEY, 1842-44.

The year 1842 was a very active one both at Horkesley and Windsor. At Horkesley, with the co-operation of his curate Mr. Holland, the parish duties were brought into excellent working order, and the Rector was elected Guardian for the parish, the duties of which post he continued to discharge regularly and actively for the rest of his life. Hitherto there had been no house for the curate, but in this year David Markham bought a convenient house situated nearly in the centre of the parish, with some land, all of which he intended to devote to uses connected with the good of the parishioners. The house on the right hand side of the causeway, with a small lawn in front and high laurels concealing it from sight, had a dining room, sitting room and offices on the ground floor, and five bedrooms above. The title deeds show that it was built in about 1788 by one John Potter, and called "Ramkins." He sold it to Nathaniel Sebborn who passed it on to Thomas Scripson the butcher in 1800, and it subsequently passed through the hands of Sarah Moore (1801), Thomas Whitmore (1816), William Burgess a grocer of Colchester (1831) and in 1833 a chemist of Colchester bought it for £335. His name was James Holiday. On the 15th of April 1842 Mr. Markham bought the house called "Ramkins," but which Mr. Holiday had christened "Vine Cottage," a parcel of land of 6 rods called "Sayers," 3 acres of land called "Worlocks," a piece of waste marked No. 49 on the plan of the parish – of 14 perches, and another of 5 perches, marked No. 42, for the sum of £700. In the first place this purchase was a great gain in supplying a good residence in the centre of the parish, so that the Rector and Curate were thus enabled to arrange the visiting with more regularity, and also to provide more efficiently for occasional classes and lectures.

The Windsor residence of 1842 was during June and July, and David Markham was busily engaged in making arrangements for executing restorations in St. George's Chapel, his Coadjutor being Mr. Cust. The architect they selected for the work was Mr. Thomas Willement F.S.A. The eastern windows of the clerestory of the choir were re-glazed in rich and powerful colours, the whole of the west window of the nave was rebuilt and stained glass figures of the time of Henry VII were replaced with improved accessories, and the coats of lime wash were removed with great care from .... (page missing)

...improvements were made to the organ itself. In 1843 the ground in front of the west end of the chapel was lowered, a handsome flight of stone steps took the place of an untidy grass slope, and catacombs were formed beneath.

David Markham wished also to pull down some old houses and walls so as to clear the precincts of the chapel, and he also had designs for the restoration of the Horse Shoe Cloisters and of the approaches. Although he was unable to carry his point during his life time, these improvements have since been made by Sir Gilbert Scott, almost exactly as he had intended.

The restorations at St. George's increased the beauty of that noble and interesting chapel, and will be a monument of the educated taste of those who originated and completed them.

In 1842 it was determined by the Markham Family to erect a worthy monument to Archbishop Markham in York Minster, and the design as well as the whole management was left to David Markham. After sketching several designs, and receiving others from eminent artists, he finally decided upon an alter tomb raised upon a high step with tessellated tiles. Round the sides are the arms of the Archbishop's children with their marriages, in compartments, and on the top is a polished black marble slab with a brass inscription round it, and a cross in brass with scroll and the arms of the See, etc. Salvin and Willement prepared the designs, and Raymond Smith built the tomb: the whole cost being £280. At the same time a brass tablet to the memory of the Archbishop was placed in the cloisters of Westminster Abbey. The York tomb was completed in 1844.

In 1841 Mr. Markham's eldest son David went to Westminster, the school where so many Markhams had been educated before him. Clements followed after Whitsuntide in 1842; when David got third into college. Selina had a governess at home, Miss Malleson from 1840 to 1842, Miss Ritchie until 1844, and then Miss Wanner, a Swiss of great ability who had previously been at Nunappleton, and afterwards at Asberton with Frank Foljambe.

David Markham's sixth and youngest child was born at Horkesley on the 28th of September 1842, a daughter named Gertrude Caroline Lucy. Her godfather was William Mordaunt Milner Esq., her mother's brother, and her godmothers her aunts Mrs. Wickham and Miss Caroline Milner. In the winter of 1843 the family was again visiting in Yorkshire.

In 1843 two valued friends passed away. Dr. Living of Nayland, to whose skill and unremitting care the family owed so much, died in March aged 38 and was succeeded by Mr. Fenn (a relation); and on September 1st 1843 Mr. William St. Croix, the Chapter Clerk at Windsor, died, his place filled by Mr. Batcheldor.

In March 1844 the Reverend Charles Holland[39] resigned the curacy owing to ill health, to the great regret both of the Rector and of the Parishioners. He was succeeded by the Reverend Henry Williams Baker,[40] eldest son of Admiral Sir Henry Baker Bart., who entered upon his duties on the Sunday before Christmas day

[39] Author's note: Mr. Holland became Vicar of St. Stephen's, Ipswich. On January 31st 1850 he was married at Stoke, to Miss Emily Forlesse, the daughter of the Vicar. In 1859 Lord Leconfield presented him to the Rectory of Petworth, in Sussex, a living with a population of 3304, and worth £856. He retired in 1896, and died aged 93 on April 26th 1910.

[40] Sir Henry Williams Baker (1821-18770 attended Trinity College Cambridge, where he achieved a B.A. in 1844. He was ordained in 1846 and served as Curate at Great Horkesley until 1851, when he was presented to the vicarage of Monkland, where he remained until his death in 1877. He is best known as a writer of hymns, his best known work being *Hymns Ancient and Modern* (1860). See, Susan Drain, "Baker, Sir Henry Williams, third Baronet (1821-1877)"

1844, being then aged 23 years. Mr. Holland was a great loss, and so were his charming sisters Emma, Sophia, Emily, and Henrietta, who often came to stay with him at Vine Cottage. In 1850 David Markham spoke of the two latter as "equally intelligent, agreeable, and good humoured." They contributed much to the gaiety and brightness of the society at the Rectory, which was often increased by visits of friends and relations from Windsor and Yorkshire. Indoors there were many games in the evenings, and much singing; as Miss Wanner was a good singer, and David Markham had an excellent ear and was very fond of music. Later he often joined in part songs with his daughter Selina and others. Out of doors the boys were very fond of riding, and David's favourite amusement was fishing, for perch chiefly, in the Stour and in the stream of Wiston Mill, the favourite walk from the rectory.

On April 16th 1844 Mrs Markham's brother William Milner was married to his second cousin Georgina Lumley,[41] whose mother was a daughter of the Bishop of Kilmore, brother of her grandmother Mrs. Clements; and on July 23rd of the same year Caroline Milner was married to Sir John Craven Carden Bart. of Templemore in Ireland.[42] In the same year too, Mr. Egerton moved from Dunnington to the much better living of Middle in Shropshire.[43] Henry Milner was, in those days, with a Private Tutor at Messing in Essex (Mr. Henderson an old friend and schoolfellow of David Markham at Westminster) and he very often came over to Horkesley.

Oxford Dictionary of National Biography. (Oxford: Oxford University Press, 2004) Online Ed.

[41] Author's note: She was afterwards Lady Georgina Milner, when her brother Richard Lumley succeeded to the Earldom of Scarborough in 1856. Their children were: Edith Harriet , born February 26th 1845; Evelyn Selina, born June 25th 1846; William Mordaunt, born May 10th 1848; Frederick George, born November 7th 1849; Granville Henry, born December 28th 1851; Dudley Francis, born March 9th 1854; and Edward Carolus, born February 1st 1858.

[42] Author's note: Their children are listed as being: Harriet Caroline Carden, born April 23rd 1845 at Nunappleton; Beatrice Georgina, born October 8th 1846; and Constance Laura, born May 15th 1850.

[43] Author's note: The patron was then Lady Bridgewater, and afterwards Earl Brownbow. The living was at the time worth £1003 a year, with a population of 797.

CHAPTER FIVE

MEDITERRANEAN TRAVELS

The *Achilles* was a steamer of 1000 tons and 450 H.P. belonging to the P. and O. Company and intended to run between England and Trebizonde. She had lately been bought from the Glasgow and Liverpool Company, and this was her first long sea voyage, for which she was not very well prepared. There was much carving and gilding, and painted panels with scenes from the life of Achilles; but the table was badly supplied. For the first two or three days there was a strong head wind and choppy sea, and nearly all the passengers were ill; but they recovered when the steamer got into a smooth sea and fine weather off the coast of Portugal.

David Markham, and his son, were the first to come on deck, already feeling the benefit of the change of air and scene. The former was immensely amused with one of the second class passengers whom he heard talking broad Yorkshire, and with whom he got into conversation.

> I enquired of him whether he had been much of a traveller. He said he had never been further than Bradforth. Where are you going? To Constantinople. What to do there? Whoy E' 'Sultan's agate a setting oop a factory. I'se boon to gang as foreman. He's gotten slobbers and piecers and spinners, and E' things been agate happen this two or three year, and he's offered me a matter of E' thick eend o' two hundred pound a year to larn E' Turks to mak their awn claithes. The whole thing was so rich, it made me roar with laughter, even in the midst of my misery.

The *Achilles* arrived at Gibraltar on the 26th, and the party landed at the old mole to see the various parts of the rock, the town, and Europa point. One great pleasure, in this excursion, was to find that the change had already done good to the invalid. David Markham writes:

> Only imagine Kate, who never walked beyond the kitchen garden at Horkesley, positively surmounting some of the steeps of this precipitous rock, trampling down prickly pears, brushing past powerful aloes, and all this in a violent shower of rain, and regaining the carriage without any serious effects from the unusual exertion.
>
> * Editor's Note: (Here there are a series of pages missing, quite possibly removed for the water colours of the Maltese landscape that originally accompanied the text. The text continues with their arrival in Sicily).

In the evening of the 24th of February 1846 David Markham embarked on board the Sicilian steamer *Maria Christina*, and left Malta with Colonel and Mrs Stuart, for a tour in Sicily. The next morning they landed at Syracuse, and passed six hours in visiting the cathedral, the amphitheatre, the ear of Dionysius, the tombs of Archimedes and Timoleon, and the church of San Giovanni, "a curious and ancient structure partaking of the Norman style, with a beautiful rose window of the 14th century." Hoping to make a closer examination of Syracuse on his way back to Malta, the party returned to the steamer, and arrived at Catania in the same afternoon, where they went ashore.

Next morning the first visit was to the Benedictine Convent, which "is very fine, with a handsome double marble staircase leading to noble open corridors that look out upon the most charming gardens in the different quadrangles. The largest, however, is outside the building, and commends, from among rows of cypresses, beautiful views of Etna." Next they went to the cathedral, "on the site of one built by Count Roger, of the ancient church only the three apses at the east end remain, showing evident Norman work. The western façade is adorned with granite pillars taken from the ruins of the theatre." In the afternoon David Markham, with the Stuarts, drove to Monte Rosso, a distance of 12 miles of continuous ascent through groves of orange and olive trees. At the village of Nicoloso they took mules to continue the ascent to the crater, which was accomplished without much difficulty. "We were well rewarded when the magnificent view from the top broke upon our sight. On one side was Etna, Paterno and its Norman keep and N_isser Bianco, well backed by the range of mountains that traverses Sicily from north to south, and on the other the whole Calabrian coast. I made a drawing of this scene as well as my giddy head would allow, and also one of the crater with Catania in the distance. Mrs Stuart proved herself one of the most active as well as the most diligent and enthusiastic sight-seers I ever met. We got back to Catania late in the evening."

On the 27th of February the party left Catania in a veturino,[44] for Messina, stopping the night at Giardini for the purpose of visiting the magnificent site of ancient Faorminium. The first place they passed, after leaving Catania, was Aci Castello prettily situated on the sea coast with a very picturesque castle on a projecting tongue. Here was the site of the port of Ulysses, and of the fable of Acis and Galatea, and from the former the place takes its name. Half an hour afterwards they passed through Aci Reale, stopping to see the church. Mr Markham noted, while abroad, the positions of churches with reference to the rule that the altar and chancel must be to the east. In Valetta, as the streets are at right angles, running east and west, and north and south, and as there are churches in almost every street, with entrances to the street, there are as many chancels facing to the north, south and west, as to the east. At Aci Reale the church was built N.E. and S.W. by compass. From this place they passed through a rich country to Giarre, with very fine olive trees. Mr Markham jumped over a wall to measure one which was upwards of 16 feet in girth, breast high.

> On leaving Giarre every step we took increased in beauty and variety, and this to such a degree, all the way to Giardini, that the

[44] The Oxford English Dictionary defines Veturino as "a person hiring out carriages or horses, a driver of a Vettura." Therefore the author appears to have his terms confused, and meant to say Vettura. Lesley Brown (Ed.), *The New Shorter Oxford English Dictionary*. Vol. 2. (Oxford: Clarendon Press, 1993) p. 3572.

> traveller is lost in astonishment at the multiplicity of fine and remarkable objects that everywhere surround him. The outline of the mountains upon one peak of which is Faormeria, and on another and a higher one Mola, while at their foot is Giardini. The sea and coast of Calabria on the one side, and the rich slopes of the nearer hills on the other, clad with corn and vines, olives and oranges, and fields of flax in full flower: the whole forms a scene that no description, no painting could convey, and must be seen to be at all appreciated.

They reached Giardini in the evening, and found it to be a wretchedly dirty little fishing town.

> There appeared to be no place whatever where we could put up for the night, and to our consternation the carriage stopped at a house that infinitely surpassed our most lively surmises, and we were told that this was the *Albergo*. Mrs Stuarts courage fairly gave way, and when the old brigand who kept the hostelry most politely invited us to enter, she exclaimed in despair – 'I cannot go in'. Following the landlord through a low and filthy kitchen full of very ill-looking muleteers, we came up a rickety staircase to three cock lofts in which there were four beds. The horror that had nearly overcome Mrs Stuart only lasted for a minute, and on our return she assumed an air of cheerfulness and even fun that only the most imperturbable good humour and a high sense of the ridiculous could have produced. We soon laughed our miseries out of countenance.

At 6 o'clock of the 28th Mr Markham was up and out sketching; and at 8 they set out for Faormiria, a distance of a mile and a half up a steep ascent. The entrance to Faormiria is through an ancient Norman gateway, flanked by walls probably of the same date, overhanging a precipice.

> The first thing that attracts attention, and it is very striking, is the singular mixture of the Norman and Saracenic architecture. The Chiesa Madre is a handsome structure with considerable Norman remains, boasting of two remarkably pretty rose windows of the 14th century, and a Saracenic – Norman door very elegantly worked. The roof is supported by two rows of granite pillars that have been taken from the theatre. On one side of the piazza there

> is a very curious building that has the appearance of an ancient hospitium. Its general features are the curious mixture of Norman Saracenic that are so remarkable in most parts of Sicily. It is built round a court yard, in the interior of which is a staircase leading to a small door with an ogee beading, on the parapet of which is carved in bold rough work, a design in three compartments, of Eve springing from Adam's side, the temptation, and the expulsion from paradise. On a label near, but not connected with it, is the following legend – '*Esto michi Locu Retuigii*'. I made two drawings, and then went to the theatre.
>
> The theatre occupies a noble position, being built in a sort of natural hollow, on the summit of a projecting spur of the same mountain on which the town itself stands. Independent of the antiquarian delight such a work of former ages conjures up, the view is so varied and so sublime that the spectator is wrapped in astonishment. Imagine what the ancient Greeks beheld when enjoying the spectacle immediately before him! When he lifted up his eyes from the stage he would see, towering over his head, heights of fantastic forms crowned with picturesque buildings. Below him the deep blue of the Mediterranean, and the whole line of coast from hence to Syracuse: the Calabrian mountains on the one side, and the coast of Naxos on the other, with Mola and its fortress towering aloft, and the vast mass of Etna to back the whole. Turning his head he would look up the straits of Messina, with Rheguim on one side, and the bold cliffs and richly wooded banks on the other. It is perfect enchantment, and if one ever could fancy an earthly paradise, this would be the scene of it. The theatre itself is of vast size, and the area is strewn with broken shafts, capitals, and mouldings.

After visiting some other points of interest, they joined the carriage about two miles outside Giardini and continued the journey to Messina. At two they stopped to bait the horses at a small village called Maria del Zia di San Paolo, where there is a picturesque old tower, and they arrived at Messina towards evening, stopping at the *Albergo Victoria* in the Strada Ferdinanda.

The next day, March the 1st, was a Sunday. They had intended to go by steamer to Palermo, but the vessel had stopped running, and at last it was determined to return to Catania and proceed thence to Palermo, across the interior of the island. Mr Markham was much interested in the cathedral at Messina, and especially admired the elaborate west door. The dog tooth and chevron ornaments[45] prevail on the mouldings, and on either side are two elegantly wrought and highly enriched buttresses which run up the whole façade and stand out quite clear of the building. He also admired the churches of San Gregorio and La Madonna della Scala.

On March the 3rd the travellers went to the telegraph on the mountains above Messina, to enjoy the view.

> Nothing could be more delicious than the drive. Almost immediately on leaving the town we began the ascent, at first through gardens and vineyards, and then among brushwood and stone pines: also gum-citrus, oleander, that elegant plant the asphodel, and the bright sunny pome d'oro with its golden fruit and crisp prickly leaf, and over these waved cypress, chestnuts and oaks. On reaching the summit all of a sudden the north coast of Sicily presents itself, the sea studded most beautifully by Stromboli and the rest of the Lipari Islands. From the top of the Montagna di Castania the view of the Faro is most magnificent, with the whole coast of Calabria, and the exact form of the harbour of Messina.

On the 4th of March they commenced their eventful journey in an open caleche[46] with three horses; and, as they posted, they had no occasion to stop again at Giardini, but reached Catania at 5 the same evening.

Next day the journey across Sicily was commenced,

> Travelling along a lava road, black and grimy, and very much such a one as may be seen in the neighbourhood of our coal pits: and this it is that gives Catania so dismal an appearance, for being built of black material and plaistered over, the color of the lava penetrates the plaister, and gives it an appearance of dampness which really is not the case.

---

[45] Dog-tooth and chevron ornaments were both heavily employed in Norman and early English architecture. The term dog-tooth refers to a stone ornament with four leaves radiating from a raised central point. A Chevron is a V shaped decoration. See, Lesley Brown (Ed.), *The New Shorter Oxford English Dictionary*. Vol. 1. (Oxford: Clarendon Press, 1993). Pp. 383, 722.

[46] A Caleche was a light low-wheeled carriage with a removable folding hood. *Webster's English Dictionary.* Concise Edition. (Toronto: Strathearn Books Ltd., 1997) p. 39

We began our journey under favourable auspices and a more interesting and delightful one it would be impossible to imagine, not only from the agreeable qualities of my companions, but also from the beauty of the scenery and the loveliness of the weather.

One of the peculiarities of this mountainous region is the numerous towns and villages that are to be seen cresting the distant heights, many of them at least 3000 feet high, and giving a character to the scenery as interesting as it is uncommon. The country, as we advanced, increased in loveliness, the nearer mountains carpeted with flowers among which shone the mary gold and anemone pulsatilla in great profusion, and a very bright colored purple vetch, and over the flowers the finest olive trees I ever saw. The appearance of Etna is more majestic from the interior of the island than from the sea, owing perhaps to the high land over which the road leads and whence the traveller is enabled to see the very base of this stupendous volcano, while at sea many lower mountains intervene.

Passing through the villages of Adernio, Sistra, Ragalbuto and San Filippo d' Argiro, they stopped for the night in a wretched albergo at Leoforte.

One thing that it is impossible not to remark throughout Sicily is the custom of leaving what are called the Puttock holes in a building unstopped up, after the scaffolding is removed. This I remarked first at Syracuse, and it is universal. It may be done for effect, but gives the air of great slovenliness.

On March 6th they continued their journey, passing through Castro Giovanni, to Valle Lunga where they passed the night.

Castro Giovanni, the ancient Enna is famous in classic history as the place where Pluto is fabled to have carried off the fair daughter of Ceres. Ovid describes it, as does Cicero in his speech against the infamous Verres, who carried off the bronze statue of Ceres from her celebrated temple built on this rock, the beauty of which he extols in the most glowing terms. We were by no means disappointed after the steep ascent to the old Roman gateway of Enna. The south front of the church of Castro Giovanni is certainly early Norman and very beautiful, the dog tooth and chevron ornaments prevailing on the mouldings throughout.

> The remains of the castle convey a good notion of the mode of life of a Norman Baron of the time of Count Roger. The site of the castle and town is magnificent in the extreme.

Continuing their journey they began gradually to leave the volcanic region, and came by degrees upon limestone and marble, with a wild and steep down country, affording abundant pasturage to goats and cattle. "We passed several carts of brimstone which were gaily painted, with mules decked out with every colour of the rainbow on their trappings." Passing San Caterina and landro, they reached Valle Lunga late in the evening.

Almost the whole population of the Valle Lunga is composed of robbers, and the people of the filthy albergo looked forbidding and truculent. A pretty slipshod girl attended on them, and was most urgent that they should keep their doors locked. On wishing Mrs Stuart good night and shutting the door, she re-opened it, thrust in her head and, making a motion of silence, said in a whisper 'I will protect you'. David Markham's room had a dark passage opening on it, which led no one knew whither, and there was no fastening to the door. The night passed, however, without any event, and they were in the carriage again by 6 in the morning of the 7th of March. After having taken their last glance of Etna somewhere near Villafrati, the city of Palermo opened in their view at about 3 in the afternoon.

> We were descending a wide gorge in the mountains. The scene was most lovely, and if ever I were driven to live out of my own country, I should be inclined to select Palermo as the place to rest in. The city is in a fertile plain at the bottom of the bay, with two splendid headlands forming its extreme points, Monte Pelegrino to the west, and Cape Zaffarano to the east, backed by the most singularly formed mountains.

Colonel and Mrs Stuart and Mr Markham established themselves at the *Trinacria* Hotel, and staid at Palermo from the 7th to the 16th of March.

> The city of Palermo is large and well built, divided into four quarters by two long and handsome streets, the Via Toledo and the

> Via Macqueda intersecting each other in the centre at a spot called the Quattro Cantoni which is an eight sided piazza, possessing some pretence to architectural beauty. The number of conventual buildings, with their grills, is a striking feature of the town.

On the 8th they walked in the Villa Giulia and on the Marina, enjoying the beautiful views. On the 9th they went to the cathedral,

> …a noble and interesting pile of the 12th century: a fine specimen of Saracenic taste effected by Norman hands. The mosaic work is very magnificent, and the roof is supported by what is so common in Sicily, handsome marble pillars, the spoil of some Grecian temple.

Thence they visited the Palazzo Reale where "the staircase is very striking from the number of its round headed arches supported by slender marble pillars."

Afterwards they drove to Monte Reale by an excellent road through a rich plain covered with orange and lemon trees. Here the cathedral is the great object.

> It was built by William the Good, and is one of the most glorious specimens of Byzantine taste that is to be met with anywhere. A colossal figure of the Saviour in mosaic, filling the whole of the apse, is very fine, and the nave and choir are entirely encrusted with mosaic. Here too are porphyry sarcophagi containing the ashes of William the Bad and William the Good.

On the 10th Mr Markham visited and carefully examined several other churches in Palermo, recording his impressions and architectural criticisms in his journal, and also went to the interesting Museum of the Universities. He admired there,

> A very beautiful group in bronze of Hercules holding down a stag, found at Pompeii. The symmetry of both figures is perfect, and the display of strength and determination on the part of the man are very grand. It is a *chef d' oeuvre.*

In the afternoon the party determined to ascend Monte Pelegrino, where are the grotto and statue of S. Rasalia, the patron saint of

Palermo. The ascent occupied two hours and, including a visit to St. Rosalie's grotto, was very interesting. The 13th was spent in a careful examination of La Zuja, a genuine Saracenic building, and of La Cuba, another edifice of the same character. The 14th saw them at the monastery of San Martini, in a gorge of the mountains about 3 miles behind Monreale; and at Ponte del Ammiraglio, the work of Count Roger's High Admiral. During their stay at Palermo, they were a good deal with Lord and Lady Brabazon,[47] and Sir William and Lady Ingleby.[48]

On the 16th David Markham, with the Stuarts, embarked on board the Neapolitan steamer *Stromboli*, reaching Naples the next day; where they met the Bridgeman Simpsons who accompanied them, in the same steamer, back to Malta. On the 17th and 18th Mr Markham spent several hours at the Museo and picture gallery. The statuary gallery gave him most pleasure. At noon on the 18th he embarked on board the *Maria Christina* with his old acquaintances the Bridgeman Simpsons, very agreeable companions.[49] The steamer touched at Pizzo, on the coast of Calabria, Messina, Catania, and Syracuse, and anchored in Valetta harbour in the morning of the 22nd of March. He found his son looking better than when he had left him a month before, and the rest of the family well.

This Sicilian tour was a source of great pleasure both at the time, and afterwards. Having carefully studied Gally Knight, and the Sicililian historians Palmeri and Amari, he was able to enjoy

---

[47] Author's note: Lord Brabazon, born in 1803, was the eldest son of the 10th Earl of Meath by a daughter of the Earl of Clanwilliam. In 1837 he married Harriot, daughter of Sir Richard Brooke Bart. of Norton Priory in Cheshire, and succeeded his father as Earl of Meath in 1851. His son Lord Brabazon was born in 1841.

[48] Author's note: Sir William Ingleby was born in 1783, was eldest son of Sir John Ingleby of Ripley in Yorkshire, who was created a Baronet in 1781. Sir William married, in 1822, Louisa daughter of John Atkinson Esq., and secondly, in 1843, Mary Anne Clemertson. He died childless in 1854.

[49] Author's note: Reverend William Bridgeman Simpson, Rector of Babworth, born in 1813. In 1837 he married Lady Frances Fitzwilliam, and had seven children: Orlando 1838, William 1843, George Arthur 1846, Francis Charles 1848 (later Admiral), Mary, Caroline and Beatrice.

thoroughly the historical associations; while his love of fine scenery and of architecture gave an interest to every day; the enjoyment being enhanced by congenial companionship.

Greece and Constantinople

On his return to Malta David Markham found that the flag ship was about to sail for Greece and Constantinople, and the Admiral, Sir William Parker,[50] asked him to come, with his son, as his guests on board the *Hibernia*. He gladly accepted the invitation, and went on board in the morning of the 28th of March.

> At about 11 o'clock the great ship got under weigh with a fresh breeze, gracefully floated down to the mouth of the harbour, swept round the fort of Ricasoli, and shaped her course to the eastward with the *Syren* in company. And now I was doing what for years I had longed for, taking a cruise in a three decker. The Admiral's kindness in looking after our comforts is very great, and we have both handsome cabins.

At daylight on the 30th they were off Cape Matapan, on the 1st of April they passed through the narrow channel between Cerigo and Cape St. Angelo, and anchored in the bay of Salamis on the 4th. Sir Edmond Lyons came on board, and hospitably offered the use of his house to the Admiral and his guests; and they proceeded to the Piraeus in the *Bloodhound*.

On reaching Athens no time was lost in visiting the principal points of interest, the Acropolis, the Parthenon, and the temple of the unwinged Victory,

[50] Sir William Parker, first Baronet (1781-1866), entered the navy in 1793 and served in the West Indies, the Channel and North Sea, China and the Mediterranean. In 1830 he was promoted to the rank of Rear-Admiral, and in 1841was appointed Commander-in-Chief in China. In 1845 he was appointed Commander-in-Chief in the Mediterranean. It was during this busy tour of duty that he extended his hospitality to David Markham. Parker would take a second term as Commander-in-Chief of the Mediterranean in 1849, only returning to England in 1852. J.K. Laughton, "Parker, Sir William, First Baronet (1781-1866)" *Oxford Dictionary of National Biography*. (Oxford: Oxford University Press, 2004) Online Ed.

> As elegant a little bijou as can be conceived, and containing one of the most lovely pieces of bas relief I ever saw – a victory untying his sandal. It is perfectly alive with grace, modesty, and ease. On our return we saw the temple of Jupiter Olympius; and the arch of Hadrian, which seems only useful as a contrast in point of taste to its brilliant neighbour.

At dinner, at Sir Edmund Lyons's house, David Markham sat next to General Church,[51] and had much conversation on the present state and prospects of Greece. Early in the morning of the 5th of April he climbed to the summit of Mount Lycabettus from the side facing the Ilissus.

> It was very fine to see the sun first gild the distant hills of the Peloponnesus, then lighten up Aigina and Salamis, and finally bring out the Acropolis and surrounding country in most brilliant relief.

He visited the temple of Theseus on his way back, and went afterwards to the tomb of Cymon, the Pryx, the Areopagus, and the Acropolis again.

At dinner with Sir Edmund Lyons, on April 5th, he next met Lord Bernard Howard,[52] Mr Weld-Blundell,[53] Clive, the French Admiral Turpin, and his flag Captain.

---

[51] Sir Richard Church (1784-1873). General Church was born in Cork and, bent on a career in the army, ran away from school to enlist in 1800. He rose through the ranks during the Napoleonic Wars where he saw action in Egypt, Capri and Naples, and elsewhere. In 1820 he was made Commander-in-Chief of Sicily, and would spend most of his professional life in the Mediterranean. He played an active part in the Greek Revolution and in 1854 was made a General of the Greek Army. General Church is an excellent example of Philhellenism, a movement that developed during the Greek revolt of the 1820s which saw the likes of Byron and others develop strong sympathies to the plight of the Greek people in their bid to break free from the control of the Persian Empire. H.M. Stephens, "Church, Sir Richard (1784-1873)" *Oxford Dictionary of National Biography*. (Oxford: Oxford University Press, 2004) Online Ed.

[52] Author's note: Lord Howard was brother of the 14th Duke of Norfolk who married Sir Edmund Lyon's daughter in 1839. Lord Bernard was born in 1825, and died on December 21st 1846.

[53] Author's note: Mr Weld-Blundell was second son of Mr Weld of Lulworth, who took the additional name of Blundell and succeeded to Free Blundell at Lancaster. He married Miss Vaughan in 1839, and had ten children.

The 6th was the anniversary of the liberation of Greece, the ships fired salutes, and Otto, with his Queen, reviewed the troops. David Markham, with the Admiral and Sir Edmund Lyons, went to the temple of Theseus, the Agora, and the temple of the Winds. At dinner he met Mavrocordato, Tricoupi, and other Greek Patriots, sitting next the former at Sir Edmund's request. He gave a lamentable account of the present state of Greece.

On the 7th Mr Markham was up at 5, to go up Mount Pentelicus, which took eight hours. From this point he made a sketch of the plains of Marathon and the island of Eubea.

It was arranged that on the 8th he should go in H.M.S. *Bloodhound*, with Lord Bernard Howard, to see the islands of Aegina and Poros; and they dined the night before on board the *Hibernia* meeting Captain's Glascock[54] of the *Tyne* and Edgell of the *Syren*. In the *Bloodhound* they went through the beautiful bay of Eleusis to Aegina, and soon afterwards landed on the island of Poros. They walked for two miles among the orange and lemon groves in Monastery Bay; and then went across to Aegina, landing at the foot of the hill upon which the temple of Minerva stands, and climbing to the summit in time to see a most glorious sunset.

Returning to Athens on the 10th, David Markham made a more minute examination of the Acropolis.

> The view of the bay of Salamis through the Propylaea I still think the most striking point. The masonry is one of the things that ought not to be passed unnoticed. It is almost impossible to distinguish the joints of the stones; and the surfaces of the ends of the drums of the pillars appear to have been polished before they were laid one upon the other.

---

[54] William Nugent Glascock (1787?-1847) entered the navy in 1800 and saw service in the Baltic, the West Indies, at Newfoundland, off the Irish coast and the Mediterranean. He commanded the frigate Tyne from April 1843 until January 1847, when he left the Mediterranean for Ireland, where he died suddenly on 8th October 1847. J.K. Laughton, "Glascock, William Nugent (1787?-1847)" *Oxford Dictionary of National Biography*. (Oxford: Oxford University Press, 2004) Online Ed.

At dinner he again met General Church, who talked a good deal about his brother-in-law William Mure, the greatest of British Greek scholars.[55] In the evening he went with Sir Edmund Lyons, Lord Bernard Howard, and Captain Edgell to see the Acropolis by moonlight, starting at 10 and not returning until 1 in the morning. "This was my last visit to the Parthenon and temple of Jupiter, whose like I shall never see again."

On the 12th of April the *Hibernia* got under weigh, beating out against a foul wind, with the *Virago*, *Tyne*, *Syren* and *Bloodhound* in company. The Admiral was kindly anxious that David Markham should see the temple of Sunium both by daylight and moonlight, and therefore ordered the *Virago* to take him to the cape, arriving there an hour before sunset.

> I never witnessed a more glorious scene, looking upon the Peloponnesus and the islands near it, with the white marble temple in the foreground. Certainly the ancient Greeks knew as well how to select the best sites for their public buildings as to build them in the best taste and symmetry.

They returned to the *Hibernia* in the night.

General Church also took a passage in the flag ship, and, in several conversations with David Markham, he gave him a very interesting account of the exertions of the Greeks to free themselves from Turkish Thraldom. All the 16th they were becalmed off Cape Doro, the ancient Cephareus promontory where a portion of the Greek fleet was wrecked on their return from Troy. Mr Markham

[55] William Mure (1799-1860), born in Ayrshire, was educated at Westminster School, the University of Edinburgh and in Germany at the University of Bonn. He began publishing at the age of 22 and went on to publish a wide variety of works on ancient Egypt and Greece. At the time of David Markham's dinner with General Church, William Mure had recently published (1842) a *Journal of a Tour in Greece and the Ionian Islands*. His greatest work, however, was his *Critical History of the Language and Literature of Ancient Greece*, published in five volumes between 1850 and 1857. See, W.W. Wroth, "Mure, William (1799-1860)" *Oxford Dictionary of National Biography*. (Oxford: Oxford University Press, 2004) Online Ed.

made a sketch of it for General Church, and another for his own collection.

On the 18th there was at last a strong southerly breeze, and the *Hibernia* was soon staggering under all the canvas she could carry. The plains of Troy soon became visible, backed by Mount Ida. Then were seen the tumuli of Achilles and Patroclus, and very soon after the entrance to the Dardanelles. The breeze continued to freshen, the topsails were double reefed, and soon afterwards the main top gallant sail was carried away.

> It was a beautiful sight to see about fifty sail of vessels all taking advantage of this favourable breeze, and bursting together into the waters of the Dardanelles. The *Hibernia* however, took and kept the lead, the *Virago*, with all sail set and steaming her utmost, being unable to close upon us.

The flag ship anchored at Gallipoli; and on the 19th of April the Admiral and his guests went on board the *Virago* and proceeded to Constantinople; where a very pleasant week was passed.

> The Turkish burial ground is a singularly lovely spot, dotted with the finest cypresses and commanding two most beautiful views of the Bosphorus. The scene was so calm and lovely, and the atmosphere so clear with the spring tints of green just suffusing the trees, that I could have loitered about it for hours. I never saw anything of the kind more enjoyable in my life. This is what constitutes the great beauty of Constantinople. Within the walls all is poor, mean, and dirty. But the general views of it from some neighbouring eminence present scenes of loveliness that cannot be described.

On the 21st he visited the slave market, the Bazaar, the Seraglio gardens, the Egyptian obelisk of Theodosius, and the pillar that supported the tripod in the Temple of Delphi. At dinner with Sir Stratford Canning[56] he met General Jochmus, formerly Aide de

[56] Stratford Canning, Viscount Stratford de Redcliffe (1786-1880), first cousin of Prime Minister George Canning. Stratford Canning was a well-travelled diplomat who spent time in Switzerland, the United States and the Mediterranean. He was appointed to Constantinople during the Greek Revolt (1825-1829), and

Camp to General Church in the Greek war of liberation. On the 22nd the Firmian obtained for the Admiral admitted them to the Mosque of St. Sophia, the Seraglio, and the Seven Towers. On the 23rd they crossed the Hellespont to Scutari, and rode thence to see the view from the Bulgreau mountain, a fine gallop on magnificent turf.

> On one side the sea of Marmora and its islands with Olympus in the background, on another Constantinople and its thousand domes and minarets, the Bosphorus and the mountains that border the Black Sea. I was enchanted with the scene.

On the 24th they went to see the Sultan go to Mosque, and then, with Sir Stratford Canning, to the sweet waters of Europe, a secluded valley at the head of the Golden Horn. On the 25th they had a charming drive to Buyukdere and Bagdsche Koi, seeing the aqueducts of Sultan Mahmoud, and the tanks which supply Pera and Galata with water. After luncheon at Buyukdere they crossed over to Anatoli Kawak, and ascended the giant's mountain, whence the view is almost as fine as from Buguru. On the 26th they went to the arsenal with the Admiral, and went on board the *Mahmoudieh,* where they were received in state by the Capitan Pasha, smoking chibuks and drinking coffee with him. David Markham renewed his acquaintance with Mrs Wellesley (Lady Cowley), dining with the Ambassador, and finishing the evening at the Wellesleys.

On the 27th of April David Markham and his son went on board the French steamer *Telemache* which got under weigh from the Seraglio Point at 6 p.m. with a delightfully calm sea and beautiful setting sun. Passing the plains of Troy, Tenedos, and

---

after a brief stint at domestic politics in Britain, returned in 1842. It was during this stay (1842-1846) that David Markham had the opportunity to dine with him. He would return to Constantinople later in his career, but is perhaps best known for his controversial part in the outbreak of the Crimean War in 1854. Muriel E. Chamberlain, "Canning, Stratford, Viscount Stratford de Redcliffe (1786-1880)" *Oxford Dictionary of National Biography*. (Oxford: Oxford University Press, 2004) Online Ed.

Mytilene, they ran along close in shore. "Many most tempting places presented themselves, where one's imagination fancied a life of most innocent delight and pleasure. One monastery was exquisitely situated, and must command a glorious view." On the 29th the *Telemache* dropped anchor in the harbour of Smyrna, and they had four hours to explore the place before the steamer started again. They rode up to the old castle whence there is a magnificent view of the town and gulf, and then visiting the bazaars. At 10 a.m. they were steaming out again, and enjoyed the view of the coast, and of the island of Chios. On the 30th the steamer touched at Piroeus, and reached Malta on the 3rd of May, where they were obliged to undergo a wearisome quarantine of six days. This afforded time to finish the numerous sketches that had been made during the cruise; and every day that had been made during the cruise; and every day there were visitors; his wife and daughter, Lady and Miss Duncan, the Miss Parkers, Lord Charles Hervey,[57] Captain Galton[58] and others, whose conversation served to while away the hours. On the 8th they were released from quarantine, and on the 14th of May the whole party, with Lady and Miss Duncan, left Malta in the Neapolitan steamer *Ercolano*, on their way home.

[57] Lord Arthur Charles Hervey (1808-1894), Bishop of Bath and Wells. Known to be of moderate views on church matters, and with an avid interest in the promotion of educational institutions, Hervey would have much in common with David Markham. Like Markham, Hervey was attracted to archaeology and family history, publishing a chronology of Jewish History entitled *The Genealogies of Our Lord*, in 1853. William Hunt, "Hervey, Lord Arthur Charles (1808-1894) *Oxford Dictionary of National Biography*. (Oxford: Oxford University Press, 2004) Online Ed.

[58] Here the author is referring to Sir Douglas Strutt Galton, (1822-1899) an engineer who went to the Mediterranean in 1841 and was stationed at Malta and Gibraltar. He returned to Britain in 1846 and joined the Ordnance Survey, but rose to prominence through his development of sanitary engineering. His work greatly influenced the design and improvement of conditions in hospitals and army barracks. R.H. Vetch, "Galton, Sir Douglas Strutt (1822-1899)" *Oxford Dictionary of National Biography*. (Oxford: Oxford University Press, 2004) Online Ed.

The Return Home: Italy, Switzerland and the Rhine

After leaving Malta the *Ercolano* touched at Syracuse, Catania, and Messina, and arrived at Naples on the 18th of May. The Duncans landed at Catania, where they parted with the Markhams after an intimacy of seven months, which both sides determined to resume on every opportunity. At Naples the Markhams stayed at the *Crocalli* hotel, and the 19th was devoted to a long visit to Pompeii. David Markham was deeply interested in every detail of the ruins, and his pleasure was enhanced by the intelligent interest shown by his daughter Selina. He says – "Selina was very much interested. How pleasant it is to get a person, however young, to enter into these things, and express their enjoyment."

On the 20th the day was spent at Baia. Passing through the grotto of Posilippo they soon arrived at the ancient Puteoli, and got a fine view of Lake Avernus. Next they drew up under the Acro-felica whence they saw the site of ancient Cumoe. Thence they walked as far as the Tiberius Villa and the grotto of the Cumoean Sibyl, and so to Baioe; examining the relics of temples and the ruins of Caesar's villa at Puzzuoli on their return.

The 21st was devoted to the Museo.

> I am more convinced than ever of the high state of art that must have existed to produce such sketches as those found in Pompeii, and this conviction was further confirmed by the beautiful mosaics that I had not seen before, the drawing and spirit to be seen in them has never been surpassed. They are rough, it is true, but they show a master genius.

In the same afternoon they re-embarked on board the *Ercolano*, arriving at Leghorn on the 23rd, and thence making an expedition to Pisa. At Leghorn David Markham received news of the death of his old friend Dean Hobart of Windsor.

Genoa was reached on the 24th, where Lord Charles Hervey,[59] who had only arrived the day before, came on board to meet

[59] Author's note: Lord Hervey was fifth son of the 5th Earl and 1st Marquis of Bristol. He was in Holy Orders, and Rector of Great Chesterford in Essex. Born in 1814 he married in 1839 Lady Harriet Byden daughter of the Earl of Harrowby and had a large family. He died on April 11th 1880.

them; having boats ready and having taken rooms for them at the *Quatro Nazioni*. David Markham had been at Genoa 25 years before, in 1821, with his brother William.

> I think the town the handsomest, in point of street architecture, I was ever in, except Venice. The Archdeacon of Malta and Lord Charles Dined with us, and afterwards we walked in the gardens.

The 25th was given up to the churches and palaces of Genoa.

> I particularly admired, at the Palazzo Balbi, a Rubens – the subject an infant Christ and St. John playing over a lamb. The landscape is admirable, as well as the figures.

At the Durazzo palace he mentions a most charming Guido under the name of 'Roman Charity' and a Madonna and child of Andrea del Sarto. He was enchanted with the view from the Doria Palace; and adds, with pleasure, "Kate did the whole of the day's work, and even (with the stimulus of Lord Charles Hervey's arm and enticing manner) contrived to reach the gazebo on the height above the gardens." On the 26th he continued the tour of the palaces. "At the Palavicino I became further acquainted with Franceschini, a painter of great merit. There is one of his pieces, the virgin carried to heaven by angels, which is very charming." He did not consider the good effect of the alternate black and white marble of the cathedral, though the general appearance is imposing.

Having made an arrangement with a voitrerier, they took leave of Lord Charles Hervey, and left Genoa for Milan on the 27th of May, passing the first night at Novi, and the second at Pavia. At the latter place David Markham was much interested in the old castle built by Giovanni Galeezzo Visconti, and in the church of Santa Maria del Carmine, "a very good specimen of moulded brick work. I only wish, where one have not stone at hand in England, our church builders would take a lesson from the architects of this country." They reached Milan on the 29th, stopping an hour at Certosa,

> Once seen before, and of which the recollection was very vivid, especially of the beautiful cloister, so simple, so light, and yet so

> solemn, and the charming little domiciles with their gardens, for each recluse. The pictures are chiefly by Luini,[60] Perigrino, Borgognone and Procacini – all good specimens of their respective masters.

At Milan they stayed at the *Hotel Reichman.* The first visit was to St. Ambrosio, and then to Santa Maria della Grazie to see the Cenacolo.

> To some people at first sight it might produce feelings of disappointment, but the more one looks at it, the more it grows upon one, and one can almost fancy one sees it in its freshest time. Certainly no engravings have ever done it justice; and to see a perfect representation of what one wishes to imagine the countenance of our saviour to have been like, one must come to Milan to see this picture. It is much in the state it was when I saw it in 1819. Hence we went to San Vittorio al corpo, which is full of most charming pictures and frescoes by Procamini, Monceluco, and Crespi. I think the frescoes of one arch, little angels by Procamini, and the vaulting of one of the side chapels by Crespi, the most perfect things of their kind I ever saw.
>
> And now for the magnificent and gorgeous Duomo. It is splendid as a whole. But the western façade is by no means to be compared to the three other fronts, and perhaps a little spoils the general effect from want of unity of design. The effect is very striking on first entering the building, solemn without being sombre or gloomy; and the painting of the roof is so well done that one is inclined, in certain lights, to imagine it to be elaborately carved. Three windows in the flamboyant style at the east end are very grand, and some old stained glass good the more modern not without merit. The colours in themselves are fine but do not blend well, which is the point in which the old masters excelled.

On the 30th he spent some time in the Bibliotheca Ambrosiana. The Brera was under repair.

---

[60] Bernardino Luini, a Lombard painter (1480-1532) described as creating figures that bridged the gap between the sacred and the secular – giving a "religious experience that is humble and rooted in everyday reality." John T. Paoletti and Gary M. Radke, *Art in Renaissance Italy*. 2nd Ed. (London: Lawrence King Publishing, 2001) p. 345.

Sunday was spent at Como, where they heard a good sermon from the Bishop on Pentecost, in the cathedral; and they drove to Lugano on the 1st of June, and thence to Bellinizona. In crossing the Splugen, David Markham walked the greater part of the way to the summit, enjoying the sublime scenery and the variety of alpine flowers; and by 4 o'clock they had descended as far as Altdorf. Another quarter of an hour brought them to Fluellen where they took the steamer, arriving at Lucerne at half past eight in the evening of the 3rd of June. On the 5th they went by diligence from Lucerne to Basle, and thence to Manheim, the 7th being passed at Heidelberg, which David Markham had visited twice before in early days. They went down the Rhine in a steamer, and on the 9th they were at Cologne; crossing over from Ostend to Dover on the 12th of June 1846, and arriving at Horkesley on the 15th, after an absence of nearly eight months.

David Markham kept a journal while he was abroad; but the most charming memorial of his tour consists in a very complete series of water colour sketches which form, in themselves, an admirable journal. They are bound up in two large volumes. Commencing with Cape Funisterre and the rock of Lisbon, they comprise some lovely little sea pieces taken in the Mediterranean, admirable views of Valetta harbour, architectural bits in Malta and Sicily, panoramic and other general views in Sicily, Greece, and on the Bosphorus, and many carefully drawn special views of churches, and other buildings in Sicily and Italy, and of temples and other ruins in Greece.[61]

[61] In total David Markham completed 136 water colour sketches during his Mediterranean travels. These were removed from the Markham history before the present editor acquired the manuscript, and sold at Christies in 2004.

CHAPTER SIX

THE INFANT SCHOOL, PAROCHIAL WORK AND HOME EVENTS

During the summer of 1846 the whole family, except the son in the *Collingwood*, was assembled at Horkesley. Young David's health was improved, and he was able to resume his studies for Oxford, amusing himself with fishing and taking long rides. He also paid visits at Esholt, Becca and Nunappleton from August 18th to September 7th when he joined his family at Windsor. It was arranged that he should pass the winter of 1846-47 at Malta, travelling with Mr Mountain, who was to be a sort of private tutor to him. They left England on the 17th of September 1846 and David returned home on the 9th of July 1847.

The residence at Windsor was during September. Dean Hobart died on the 8th of May 1846, and was succeeded by the Honourable and Reverend George Neville Grenville, brother of Lord Braybrooke,[62] and also David Markham's old friend Lady Wenlock (Mrs Thompson) at Escrick. He was born in 1789, and was also Master of Magdalene College at Cambridge. In 1816 he married Lady Charlotte Legge, daughter of the 3rd Earl of Dartmouth, and had ten children. Their third son, the Reverend Seymour Neville, became a Minor Canon at Windsor,[63] and at the Deanery there

[62] Richard Griffin (formerly Neville) third Baron Braybrooke (1783-1858), a prominent politician and literary editor. George, his younger brother, was Master of Magdalene College, Cambridge from 1813. D.R. Fisher, "Griffin, Richard, third Baron Braybrooke (1783-1858)" *Oxford Dictionary of National Biography*. (Oxford: Oxford University Press, 2004) Online Ed.

[63] Author's note: Seymour Neville was also Vicar of Wraysbury near Windsor. In 1869 he gave up the Minor Canonry and Wraybury, and became Rector of

were three unmarried daughters, the twins Georgina and Cicely, and Harriet.[64] A very agreeable intimacy grew up between the Markhams and the Deanery, which increased the pleasure of the Windsor residence.

The Reverend Frederick Anson[65] was installed as canon of Windsor, in the place of Mr Stopford, who died on 12th December 1844, on the 11th of January 1845; and a warm friendship was formed between him and David Markham.

The last half of 1846 was a period of great activity as regards parochial work at Horkesley. The chief event was the building of an infant school. The children in this parish left school at so early an age to go to work, that some scheme was thought advisable that would afford them a longer period of instruction than from 6 or 7 to 11 or 12, give opportunities of bringing the intellect sooner into play, and imprint good moral habits at the earliest dawn of reason. Nothing appeared so likely to secure such an end as an Infant School. Accordingly David Markham determined to erect one at his own sole expense, on the land which he had bought in 1842, near the centre of the parish. The piece of land selected was close to the Curate's house, by the side of the road leading from Horkesley Causeway to Brewood Hall, 71 feet facing to the road, and 180 feet deep. For the design of the school he prepared several drawings, but eventually took it from a curious old building that stands by the way side on the road to Colchester, about three quarters of a mile from the church.

Ockham in Surrey. He married Agnes daughter of Mr Proby (Canon of Windsor) in 1859, but she died in 1860. Her sister, Miss Proby afterwards kept house for him! He retired from Ockham, and died at Butleigh Court, aged 82, December 14th 1905.

[64] Author's note: On January 17th 1854 Harriet Neville was married to the Reverend Arundel Mildmay, Rector of Lalworth in Warwickshire, afterwards of Marston in Yorkshire, and, since 1873, of Alvechurch in Worcestershire.

[65] Author's note: Mr Anson was born on March 28th 1811. He was the son of Dr. Frederick Anson, the Dean of Chester, by Mary Anne daughter of the Reverend Richard Levett, and nephew of Thomas Viscount Anson, father of the 1st Earl of Lichfield. Mr Anson became Rector of Sudbury in Derbyshire, in 1836. On May 7th 1845 he married Caroline Maria, daughter of Lord Vernon, by whom he has a large family.

This is a small oratory or Lady Chapel, now much defaced and converted into two cottages. It is built of brick, and consists of a chancel and priest's house behind it. It is of the perpendicular style with an east window now blocked up, and is supported by buttresses of good character. The wood work of the roof still remains, and there is a piscine in the south wall. On the north side, towards the west, is a good perpendicular doorway. (page missing) David Markham's fondness for children made him take a very special interest in its prosperity. The Infant School was his favourite walk, and he took great delight in showing it to visitors at the Rectory.

Another institution established at this time was a Parochial Association in aid of the Society for the Propagation of the Gospel.[66] David Markham thought that it would, while adding to the funds of a useful Society, also have the effect of exciting an interest in matters beyond the limits of every day life, and by arousing the curiosity would enlarge the minds of his parishioners. He set on foot a series of quarterly meetings in the school house, beginning in 1847, at which lectures were delivered on the various countries and peoples included in the operations of the Society. The members soon numbered from 75 to 80. The lectures were illustrated by maps, large scale views and drawings, and other diagrams all drawn by himself.[67] A lending library, the books being kept in the vestry, and issued after evening service on Sundays, had been established in 1840, and continued to flourish. In 1847 it contained 224 volumes.

Young David returned home on July 9th 1847, with his health so far restored that he was able to resume his classical studies.

---

[66] The Society for the Propagation of the Gospel was founded by Thomas Bray, founder of the Society for the Promotion of Christian Knowledge. Its aim was to better educate both settlers and the native inhabitants of Britain's colonial possessions. It was at first aimed at the American colonies and the plantations of the West Indies, but gradually expanded. See, John Cannon (Ed.), *The Oxford Companion to British History*. (Oxford: Oxford University Press, 2002) p.873.

[67] Author's note: After his death, they were given to Sir Henry Baker.

From July 30th to August 12th he was visiting at Esholt, Becca and Nunappleton, and, as he never failed to do when he was at the latter place, he rode over to Stillingfleet and Kelfield on August 12th, to see his old friends. The Windsor residence was in August and September; and on the 9th of the latter month young David went to his Father's friend Mr Owen,[68] at Colchester, to study for his matriculation. The family returned to Horkesley on the 7th of October; and on the 20th young David matriculated at Oxford, dined with old Westminster friends at Christ Church, and returned to Horkesley the next day. On the 23rd Dr Murray, the Bishop of Rochester, held a confirmation in Horkesley Church for the first time, and the next day, being Sunday, he staid at the Rectory until the 25th of October.

But young David was still very delicate, and it was settled that he should pass the winter of 1847-48 at Torquay. His uncle, Colonel Markham of Becca, was obliged to go there with his family, owing to the precarious state of the health of Adela, his third child, and David would thus have the companionship of his uncle and cousins.[69] He went to Torquay with his Father on the 30th of November 1847, the latter staying there until the 7th of December, and then returning to Horkesley.

---

[68] Author's note: The Reverend Lewis Owen was Rector of Trinity Church in Colchester, and also of Marks Tay in Essex. He lived in St. Mary's Terrace on the Lexden Road, 1870 Rector of Wonston (Hants), & Prebendary of Winchester. He died at Wonston on January 7th 1883.

[69] Author's note: Colonel Markham now had twelve children: 1. William Thomas born July 13th 1830. Married April 16th 1857 to Anne Grant. 2. Laura Elizabeth Frederica born February 1st 1829. Married October 29th 1856 to Colonel Pearson. 3. Adela, born September 24th 1831. Died June 26th 1848 at Becca. 4. Edwin born March 28th 1833. Married February 8th 1877 to Evelyn Stopford. 5. Mary born August 23rd 1835. Died January29th 1851 at Ryde. 6. Rose Georgina born August 31st 1836. Died April 18th 1851 at Ryde. 7. Francis born October 31st 1837. Married April 20th 1868 to Maria Markham. 8. Alfred born June 26th 1839. Died July 7th 1880 at Weymouth. 9. Lucy Henrietta born July 28th 1840. Married May 27th 1886 to Colonel Parry. 10. Emma born December 26th 1842. Married January 4th 1864 to Reverend Albert Smith. 11. Gervase born February 15th 1844. Married October 28th 1893 to Charlotte Renard. 12. Caroline born January 16th 1846. Died November 24th 1847 at Torquay.

On the 17th of September 1847, the Reverend Thomas Egerton, Rector of Middle, died suddenly of Scarlet fever. Thus David Markham, to his great sorrow, lost a very dear friend of whose sympathy he was always certain, and whom he could consult in every difficulty. His widow, with her seven young children, went to live in a house at Thorparch near Nunappleton. David Markham was with her at Middle, helping in all her arrangements, from the 6th to the 17th of November.

Young David remained at Torquay, with his uncle, from the 23rd of November 1847 to the 18th of May 1848; paying a visit to Sidmouth from the 6th to the 10th of April 1848; and going to see Plymouth and Devonport with his cousin Willy Markham from the 5th to the 8th of May. During April and May David Markham, with his wife and daughter Selina, were at Nunappleton.[70] In May they visited Mr Ansom at Sudbury, and during June they were all united again at Horkesley. Lady Milner and her daughter Louisa were on a visit there from the 15th to the 30th of June; and the house was never without guests until the move to Windsor. In these summers of 1847 and 1848 young David often amused his leisure hours with his favourite sport of fishing: for the last time.[71] Selina had gone back to the schoolroom for a year or two, after her return from abroad; but in the spring of 1848 she staid with Lady Elizabeth Clements, and had some gaiety at Lord de Ros's and other houses. The younger girls, Gena and Gertrude, were under their Governess, Miss Bonnor. They were excessively fond of Horkesley where they were born, Gena especially; and Gertrude was also fond of Windsor. Their greatest friend, for whom they formed a life long attachment, was Margaret Birch, the younger daughter of the Rector of Wiston; and the visits between Wiston and Horkesley were of almost daily occurrence; for Mr and Mrs Birch were also much attached to David Markham and his

[70] Author's note: He preached at Bolton Percy 14th May 1848.

[71] Author's note: He fished at Wiston Mill on July 15th; and in the Colne on September 22nd 1847. At Nayland on May 27th, at Wiston Mill on May 29th, 30, 31, June 12, 14, 17, 22, 26. August 25, 29, September 5 and October 1, 5, 6, 7, in 1848, and at Horkesley Loch on September 30th 1848. October 6th and 7th 1848 he and his sisters caught 100 perch.

wife, the intimacy of the first few years having ripened into close friendship.

The Windsor residence began in the end of June 1848, and in July the news reached David Markham of the Collingwood's arrival at Spithead, and the return of his second son after an absence of four years.

Chapter Seven

A Visit to Ireland and Life at Great Horkesley

From the 9th of July 1848, the day he heard of the arrival of the *Collingwood* at Spithead, to a few days before his death in March 1853, David Markham kept a journal with daily entries, as he had done while he was abroad in 1845 and 1846.

The return of his son Clements gave him great pleasure. He went down to Gosport on July 10th to 12th and saw him in Portsmouth Harbour, and the *Collingwood* being paid off, his son arrived at Windsor on July 21st and was there until the 14th of August. There were his journals to read, his collections of shells and curiosities to look over, and this led to the larger collection of shells, which had come from Stillingfleet, and had never been unpacked, being properly arranged in cabinets. At this time Frank Foljambe and Charlie Markham were at Eton, and they constantly came up to dine at their uncle's house in the cloisters. On August 14th young David and Clements went to pay visits in Yorkshire, returning home to Horkesley on the 23rd, where Clements stayed until he had to join the *Victory*. They were at Esholt, Nunappleton, and Becca, and of course set apart a day, August 18th, to visit their nurse Mrs Dodsworth, old Mrs Buckle, and other old friends at Stillingfleet and Kelfield.

Mrs Baillie, David Markham's favourite cousin, with her daughters May and Fanny, were at Horkesley from the 6th to the 13th of September, and young David had very pleasant walks with May Baillie round by Little Horkesley on the 11th, and on the 12th to Horkesley Loch. "Last day of the Baillies, most delightful ladylike girls – it is a great pleasure to renew our intimacy again. On the 13th they left us. David dreadfully downcast."

From the 18th to the 28th of September David Markham was obliged to visit the estate of John Clements in Ireland, in order personally to look into the state of his affairs. He took his son David with him. They slept at Bangor on the 18th, and on the 19th reached Dublin. On the 20th they went by coach to Cavan, and on by post chaise to Enniskillen where they found John Clements with his lawyer Mr Pulman. The next day they drove to Manor Hamilton, in the county Leitrim, John Clements's property, inherited from his father,[72] consisted of 6773 acres, chiefly moorland, valued now at £1702. After examining the condition of the potato crop, getting a bird's eye view of the estate from a mountain, and entering some of the worst cabins to form a judgement of the misery of the people, they retired for the night to a public house, for there is no residence on the property. In the afternoon of the 22nd the *Gale* was held by Mr Pulman, and a most extraordinary crew of ragged Irishmen produced a very fair amount of rent. David Markham says – "I am glad I made the exertion to come here, as I think my presence has been of some use to Johnny. Leaving Pulman to contest several agricultural points with one Mik McMurragh, we set out for Dublin on the 23rd of September." The 60th Rifles were at Dublin, and he rode with his cousins Henry Holbech and Edward Bowles who were in it, dining with them in the evening. He returned so as to reach Horkesley by the 28th, to keep his daughter Gertrude's birthday. His son Clements came home from October 13th to 16th, and then set out to join the *Bellerophon* for a passage to the *Sidon* in the Mediterranean.

[72] Author note: The Right Honourable Nathaniel Clements married Hannah, daughter and heiress of the Rev. William Gore, Dean of Down, who was son of Sir William Gore and of Hannah daughter of James Hamilton of Manor Hamilton. It was thus that Manor Hamilton came to the Clements's. Nathaniel Clements had two sons, Robert created Earl of Leitrim, and Henry Theophilus who received Ashfield and Manor Hamilton. The latter left Henry, his eldest son, the estate of Ashfield, and to his second son John, John Clements's father, the estate of Manor Hamilton. His daughter was Selena (Mrs Milner) mother of Mrs David Markham.

It was arranged that young David should pass the winter of 1848-49 in Malta and Egypt, travelling with two sons of General Vyse,[73] Edward and Frank. He was visiting his cousins the Bailies, at Eastbourne, from the 8th to the 11th of November; and sailed from Southampton on the 15th, returning home again on the 10th of May 1849. "We part with him with more satisfaction than might have been expected, for he has improved so much lately."

The complicated affairs of his former ward John Clements gave him much trouble, but this he was always ready to incur, in unstinting measure for others. He had been several times to London on this business, and on the 24th of November he set out for Dublin to be a witness at a trial, for John Clements.

*Editor's Note: (page missing, story continues with the restoration of Horkesley Church).

...accordingly the ceiling, which was plainly plastered, had ribs of a good character and with suitable moulding added. The floor was re-levelled, the steps of the altar were made in stone, oak stalls were substituted for the high deal pews, the altar rail was carried more to the eastward, a new reading desk was erected, and a handsome carved oak pulpit (which had formerly stood in the church of St. Margaret at Ipswich, since the days of James I) was put up in place of an old shabby deal one. A new oak door replaced one of deal, and all the interior stone work in the chancel was repaired. The veredos was presented by Colonel Markham of Becca, with the exception of the rood work, the carved part of which originally formed some portion of the tabernacle work in York Minster. A new linen cloth and napkin for the altar were

[73] Richard William Howard Vyse (1784-1853). Vyse enjoyed a long career in the army, achieving the rank of major-general in 1846. During a visit to Egypt in 1835 he developed a passion for the countries ancient history and began exploring the pyramids. See, E.I. Carlyle, "Vyse, Richard William Howard (1784-1853)" *Oxford Dictionary of National Biography*. (Oxford: Oxford University Press, 2004) Online Ed. Vyse therefore had much in common with David Markham, as they both shared a passion for ancient history. This, and the companionship Vyse's sons would have offered young David, made this course of action very desirable.

presented by Lady Milner, a new bible and prayer book by the Rector and Church Wardens, and two corresponding altar services by Mrs David Markham. They were all used for the first time on Christmas day 1848.

In the following year, 1849, the whole of the nave was thoroughly cleaned and repaired, the white wash was removed from the timbers of the roof, and the plaister from the jambs of the windows, the arches and pillars, the hideous gallery was removed, the arch into the tower opened and the organ placed within it, and the north-east chantry was fitted with oaken benches. The old door was divested of a mass of paint, and divided into two, which made it more convenient and stronger. Except the mere cleaning and repairing, all this was done at the expense of the Rector. A new font was presented from subscriptions collected by the Curate, the Reverend H.W. Baker;[74] and the ancient wooden cover was restored and hung at the expense of the Rector.

The year 1849 opened very gloomily with respect to want of work among the labourers, there being no less than 20 working on the roads. On the 9th of January the highway rate was exhausted, and these were sent adrift. The surveyor refused to call another rate, notwithstanding the Rector's exertions to induce him to do so; and the consequence was that 16 of the men, with their wives and children, were obliged to go to the work-house, in all 44 souls.[75] The conduct of these poor people was very exemplary. David Markham, in the hope of remedying this state of affairs, called a meeting of the farmers on the 25th of January 1849, to take into consideration the means of obtaining employment on the land, the want of which was the cause of all

---

[74] See Appendix Eighteen: Clergymen at Great Horkesley.

[75] Workhouses were an Elizabethan invention designed to discipline and make productive societies able- bodied poor. The use of workhouses expanded during the 18th century and came into prominence after the Poor Law Act of 1834. This act required all of the new unions of parishes to provide a central workhouse, and the amount of outdoor relief was greatly reduced. From 1834 there was a great stigma attached to the workhouse, and many would risk starving before entering a workhouse door. John Cannon (Ed.), *The Oxford Companion to British History*. (Oxford: Oxford University Press, 2002) p.1001.

the distress. It was a crying evil, and one of long standing in the parish. The farmers were hard selfish men. At the meeting the Rector took the chair, and there were present Mr Partridge of Brewood,[76](the Rector's Church Warden), Mr Stedman (the parish Church Warden), Mr Sadler, Mr Stannard, Captain Kelso, Mr Fisher Hobbs, Mr Croydon, Mr Bibby, Mr John Green, Mr Nevard, Mr Knoff and others. In the midst of much altercation, the blame of the present state of things being thrown from one shoulder to another, it was proposed to appoint a Committee to obtain a list of all the labourers in the parish who are employed by parishioners, and to apportion the unemployed to those who do not employ their portion according to the average, all present agreeing to employ a number equal to that average. But two farmers, Stedman and Stannard, stood out against the proposal, and it was felt to be useless unless there was unanimity.

The result was that no remedy could be applied, and the poor suffered. But David Markham was convinced that the selfish farmers would also suffer eventually. No farm can be fairly managed without the labour of 4 or 5 men for each 100 acres. The labouring population of the parish is about 140,[77] and of these David Markham and Mr Sadler employed *surplus* labour to the amount of 20 men, leaving only 100 available for the necessary labour of the parish, or barely 3 per 100 acres. He exclaims, "In what state must the farming be in this parish, and what the *animus* of those to whom the comforts of the poor are necessarily entrusted!" From January to June 1849 the same state of things continued. Many fathers of families were out of work, and considerable distress prevailed in consequence. The Rector, who had continued to be elected Guardian since 1843, visited his people at the work house. On the 29th of January they all came

[76] Author's note: Mr Partridge was the Rector's Church Warden from 1838 to 1853. He was an excellent old farmer with a large family, at Brewood Hall, a farm belonging to Lord de Grey. William Partridge died on April 5th 1863, aged 77, and was buried at Great Horkesley, at the east end of the church. His wife Ann died on March 7th 1865, aged 76.

[77] Author's note: In 1851, out of the population of 747 in 164 families, 132 were occupied in agriculture.

out, and went in a body to the rectory to thank him for his kindness and his exertions for their welfare. He employed several himself, got others employment, and so the distress was mitigated until more work came with the summer.

During January, February, and part of March he suffered from recurring attacks of gout, which were particularly distressing and inconvenient during an anxious and very busy time. In these periods of enforced inaction he carefully read the Fairfax correspondence; and Lazard's Nineveh, preparatory to an examination of the Nineveh remains at the British Museum, with his sister Emma, on the 30th of April.

The *Sidon* was paid off at Portsmouth on the 1st of April, and his son Clements arrived at Horkesley the same evening, and was at home until the 27th when he joined the *Superb* at Spithead; having, on the 23rd, been confirmed by the Bishop of London at St. George's, Hanover Square. From the 1st to the 10th of May David Markham was in Yorkshire, at Becca and Nunappleton. He found his brother William in a very precarious state of health from heart disease, and that there could henceforth be nothing but painful anxiety about him. His brother John was also at Becca, for the last time. David Markham went thence to see his sister-in-law, Mrs Egerton, at Thorparch. "I found Chaddy's family very flourishing. Gena grown and improved, though looking ill. Mary a charming little girl." On the 8th of May he went over from Nunappleton to Stillingfleet to see all his old friends, and to arrange with Mr Pretyman, the Curate resident at the vicarage, about the fund that was subscribed for the survivors from the accident in the river, in 1833. Mr Pretyman drove him and Fanny Milner to Moreby where he saw old Mr Preston and his son and daughter in law. He then first made the acquaintance of young Mrs Preston, a daughter of Sir Guy Campbell and of Pamela daughter of Lord Edward Fitzgerald.

Sir William Milner had determined to build and endow a church at Acaster, near the banks of the Ouse, to save the people from the inconvenience of having to cross the river to go to church at Stillingfleet. Returning home from Moreby, David Markham inspected the site at Acaster which had been selected for the new church.

He returned to Horkesley on the 12th of May, and found that young David had reached home two days previously. He had been ill, but Dr Fenn, the Neyland medical man, pronounced a good opinion of his lungs and breathing. But he was not really better. He was taken ill again, and had no fishing nor any of his old amusements in this summer. On the 27th of June they all went to Windsor for the residence, which lasted until the 19th of August. They had visits from Sir William Milner, Gena and Laura Milner, and Mrs Egerton. On the 29th David Markham had a walk and a long conversation with his old friend Tom Fairfax of Newton Kyme. On the 30th to the 2nd of July his son Clements came up from the *Superb* on leave, and again from the 1st to the 13th of August. The last time the two brothers saw each other was at Windsor on the 13th of August 1849.

During this residence David Markham was much occupied with projects for the improvement of the chapel precincts. He proposed, but could not then carry, the demolition of several unsightly houses and walls, and drew designs for the restoration of the horse-shoe cloisters. It is remarkable that these improvements have since been carried out by Sir Gilbert Scott,[78] almost exactly as David Markham would have made them. He had a fine edition of Potes *History and Antiquities of Windsor Castle and the Royal College and Chapel of St. George* (Eton 1749), with which he bound up the account of the restorations by Willement in 1842,[79] and also several manuscript notes of his own. In these notes he brought the lists of Knights, Deans, and Canons up to date, and added many interesting pieces of information.

---

[78] Sir George Gilbert Scott was a prominent Victorian architect and designer of the Albert Memorial. Scott applied his talents to a wide range of buildings but specialized in church restoration, in which he was involved through much of his career. He passionately argued for authenticity in restoration as he believed it was too often the case that England's churches were being damaged through the application of modern ideas. See, Gavin Stamp, "Scott, Sir George Gilbert (1811-1878), *Oxford Dictionary of National Biography*. (Oxford: Oxford University Press, 2004) Online Ed.

[79] Author's note: This volume was presented to the Chapter Library at Windsor by his son, on June 17th 1881.

After leaving Windsor, the family paid a round of visits in Ireland and Yorkshire from August 24th to October 24th 1849, the party consisting of Mr and Mrs David Markham, their son David and daughter Selina. They passed the night of August 23rd at Conway, with which David Markham was delighted. "It is the only place I know in England, in which one can completely realize the habits of our forefathers. The castle and walls of the town are so complete, and I should imagine the houses themselves and the customs of the people to have changed as little as the aspect of the old walls." At Dublin, where they were on the 25th, Sir Edward Borough took them over the old Parliament House, the College, the Castle, Freemason's Hall, the Exchange, and Atkenson's Poplin manufactory.

In the evening of the 25th David Markham received the news that his young cousin, Henry Holbech of the 60th, was dangerously ill of small pox at the Royal Barracks. He at once went there, and his worst fears were confirmed. The Doctors forbade his entering the room, saying that it would be no use as he could not recognize anyone, and he died an hour afterwards. The regret in the regiment was very great. There was a peremptory order, in such cases, that the body should be buried at once. But David Markham determined to obtain a delay in order that some members of the family might be present. To effect this he found it necessary to see Prince George of Cambridge, whom he had known very well at Windsor in the King's time, but had not seen for 12 years. The Prince received him very cordially shaking him warmly by the hand, and gave the desired order against indecent haste in the funeral, so that the brothers might have time to come from England.

On the 27th they went to Ashfield to visit Mrs Markham's cousins, the Clementses,[80] driving from Castle Blayney Station. They staid a week at Ashfield, from August 27th to September 4th,

[80] Author's note: Colonel Clements, Mrs Markham's uncle, died on January 14th 1843. There were at Ashfield, in August 1849, his widow Mrs Clements, her sister Miss Stewart, her son Henry Clements of Ashfield, and her daughters Selina, Louisa, and Mary. They had seen a good deal of young David when he was at Rome in May 1847. Mrs Clements died on April 27th 1850.

going to Dartrey, Rathkenny, and Bellamont, and on the 31st Mr Markham was much interested in going over the union work house at Coote hill. On the Sunday, the 2nd of September, he assisted the clergyman, Mr Godfrey, preaching in the morning and reading in the afternoon. While at Ashfield he made several sketches; one of the house from the churchyard on the opposite hill; another of the lake with the church steeple showing over the trees; a third of an old pump in the valley; and a fourth of the lake at Dartrey.

This was the first time that Mrs Markham had been at Ashfield since her long visit with her grandmother, after her mother's death, when she was quite a child; and her early associations gave the place a special interest for the rest of the family.

On September 4th they went to Killadoon, in the county Kildare, to pay a visit to Lord Leitrim, staying there until the 8th; and from September 8th to October 3rd they were at Templemore, in the county Tipperary, with Sir John and Lady Carden. This was a very pleasant visit to a sister to whom they were much attached.

> On the 15th it was so fine a day that we went on expedition to Holy Cross, Caddy, Selina, David and I: a most interesting ruin, of which I made several sketches. On the 16th we went to Cashel – a most delightful day, and the ruins well worth seeing. The repairs that are in progress are of the best kind, and the Dean deserves great credit. Several sketches were the result of our visit.

While David Markham was at Becca in the previous May, the Miss Gascoignes of Parlington had pressed him very much to come and see them in their house of Cloughanodfoy, in the county Limerick.

> On September 18th went by train to Kilmallock, where I was met by the Miss Gascoignes, who made me make several sketches of the ruins there, and afterwards drove me to Coughanodfoy. The house is very good, and suited to the mountainous scenery around. They amused me tonight with their accounts of the various dangers they have encountered, and the strange adventures they met with during the insurrection, and at the time of the Irish famine. On the 19th I made a sketch of the house. They then took

> me to see the new pleasure ground made out of an impassable bog – a most marvellous creation, reflecting the greatest credit on the talent, ingenuity, perseverance and taste of my hostesses. The water, waterfalls, and growth of the evergreens are marvellous, and, backed by the mountains, this is a perfect place of enchantment. In the evening I was entertained with all their ingenious work in carving and turning; and then had a concertina accompanied by the Irish harp. Miss Gascoigne made the harp herself, after the pattern of Brian Boru's, with a double action that she has herself invented. They are certainly the most accomplished women I ever knew, united to the most undaunted courage and resolution.

On the 3rd of October 1849 the Markhams left Templemore and went from Kingstown to Liverpool, and thence to Becca. The health of Colonel Markham had become precarious, and David Markham's young godchild Mary was very ill of the same disease of which her poor sister Adela died the year before. David Markham, while at Becca, saw several of his old friends – Lord Harewood and Tom Fairfax, but it was a sad visit owing to the illness of his brother William. The eldest son William[81] had been at Eton and had joined the Rifle Brigade. The second Edwin[82] was at Woolwich, destined for the artillery; and on the 12th Colonel Markham took his third son Frank[83] up to London, to put him to school at Westminster. David Markham's visit to Becca was from the 4th to the 13th

[81] Author's note: William entered the Rifle Brigade in December 1848, and went to Canada. In December 1854 he exchanged into the Coldstream Guards. He served in the Crimea at Alma, the siege of Sebastopol, and Kertch as Aide de Camp to Sir George Brown. In 1856 he left the army. 1863 Lieutenant Colonel of the Leeds Rifle Volunteers.

[82] Author's note: Edwin became a 2nd Lieutenant in the Royal Artillery on December 19th 1850. 1st Lieutenant 1852. He served in the Crimea at Alma, Inkermann, and the siege of Sebastopol, and was engaged in the sortie on 26th October 1854. In 1857 he went to India, and was in the action of Secundra, near Allahabad, on January 23rd 1858. He returned in 1858 and went out to India again in 1864. January 1876 Lieutenant Colonel. Asst. Adjutant General at Woolwich.

[83] Author's note: Francis entered the Rifle Brigade on March 16th 1856. Lieutenant 1859. Aide de Camp to Sir A Harsford 1866. Captain 1870. He sold out in February 1872.

of October, and on the latter day he went, with his family, to Nunappleton.

The visit at Nunappleton was from the 13th to the 23rd October; and here they found Gena and Gertrude, who had been at Scarborough during their absence in Ireland.

By this time the church at Acaster was finished. On the 14th David Markham went with Sir William and Lady Milner to see it, and liked it very much. On the 17th he saw the new church at Dring Houses, near York, which he did not like so well. On the 18th he rode over to Escrick with Gena Milner, "a most cordial reception: Lady Elizabeth Lawley the most charming little person. Home after dark, in consequence of the many hands I had to shake as we passed through Stillingfleet. Had a pleasant dinner with the Harcourts at Bolton Percy.

Mr Harcourt's son Edward, with his wife Lady Susan Harcourt,[84] were going to pass the winter at Madeira; and it was arranged that young David should go with them. He was then pretty well, and went out shooting with his grandfather two or three times, without ill consequences. They returned to Horkesley on the 24th of October. From the 3rd to the 7th of November young David paid a last visit to his cousins the Baillies, of whom he was very fond, at Eastbourne, where he passed four days very happily. From the 7th to the 12th he was at home for the last time. On the 12th he started in good spirits, embarked on board the *Brilliant* at Southampton, and reached Funchal (Madeira) on the 26th of November 1849.

During this winter David Markham was more than ever occupied with business in the parish, and at Colchester. Several days in the week were always devoted to visiting the poor people, and to his work as Guardian; and besides he had to attend, and often to take the chair at Committees and other meetings in Colchester. This winter he resumed more regularly his study of the

[84] Author's note: Daughter of David Markham's old friend Lady Harriet Lascelles, born 1802, married in 1825 the Earl of Sheffield, who died in 1876. Their children were two sons, and one daughter, Lady Susan Holroyd, born 1829, married 1849 to Edward Harcourt.

Hebrew language, which he had commenced a few years before. Mr Lewis, a Hebrew scholar in Colchester, came out every week to give him lessons.

On the 7th of December Mr Markham and Mr Birch of Wiston were pall bearers at the funeral of Mr Strong, the Rector of Nyland; and on the following Sunday, the 9th, Mr Markham did the service there, before a very crowded congregation, preaching, from the text "I leave you not comfortless."

Queen Adelaide died on the 2nd of December 1849; and David Markham went to Windsor on the 12th, for the funeral, which was to be on the 13th and strictly private. He slept at Fen Hill, his aunt Lady Mansfield's house near Windsor; where his cousin Lady Caroline Murray was, to represent the Duchess of Gloucester at the funeral. At 12 o'clock on the 3rd he was in the chapter room with Mr Cust, and received Prince Albert, the Duke of Cambridge, Prince George, the two Princes of Saxe Weimar, the Archbishop of Canterbury, and many others.

> The procession formed at 10 o'clock, and as the hour struck the corpse was brought into the chapel, where ten blue jackets received it and carried it to the grave. Nothing could be more affecting than to see these fine rough fellows standing among men of the highest rank, and as much concerned and as little astonished as those around them.

After the anthem, the Archbishop of Canterbury approached the grave with Mr Markham on one side of him, and Mr Cust on the other. When the service was finished, Garter proclaimed the poor Queen's style and title, and the Chamberlain, kneeling, broke the wand of office and threw the pieces into the grave. Many were deeply affected. David Markham, who had known her intimately and felt a sincere regard for her, was much touched by this last solemn act of respect. Besides his personal regard, he respected her gentle virtues and her pious humility. She had given him a little printed account of the last illness of the King; and on the 14th of February 1850 he bought a small candlestick, at a sale of the Queen Dowager's things at Marlborough House, as a remembrance.

In the first days of 1850 the news came that one of his favourite sisters-in-law, Gena Milner, was engaged to be married to Charles Strickland, the eldest son of Sir George Strickland of Boynton. On the 3rd of February she came to Horkesley with her intended husband, and her brother William Milner. The marriage took place on the 19th of February at Nunappleton.

~ Stillingfleet church, (S. side & Moreby Chapel) and back of vicarage ~

~ Stillingfleet. Looking over the bridge ~

(houses on the right since pulled down)

Stillingfleet Vicarage

[In Mr. Markham's time there was no porch, nor bow window. The front was all grass, and flower beds, and there were several large trees. The drive came up to the end of the conservatory passage outside, and there was a wooden verandah along the front of the house]

West Window of St. George's Chapel

St. George's Chapel, Windsor. South Front

~ Views of the High Street. Colchester ~

~ St. George's Chapel. Windsor. West Front ~

– The Choir. St George's Chapel. Windsor –

– Nunappleton – North Front –
(as altered in 1860)

~ Windsor Castle from the Thames ~

Archbishop Markham's tomb. Lady Chapel. York Minster ~

~ Great Horkesley Church ~

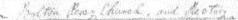

~ Bolton Percy Church, and Rectory ~

~ Bolton Percy Rectory ~

~ Great Horkesley Rectory ~

~ Nunappleton. South Front
(as altered in 1860)

~ York Minster ~

~ South door. Stillingfleet Church ~

~ St. John's Gateway. Colchester ~

~ Colchester Castle ~

This year another duty was added to all those which made up David Markham's life of ceaseless active usefulness. On the 26th of February he received a letter from the Bishop of Rochester, requesting his acceptance of the office of Rural Dean of the Deanery of Dedham, including the churches of Great and Little Horkesley, Wormingford, Boxted, West Bergholt, Dedham, and Lougham. He did not hesitate to accept the office, but his entry in his journal was "considering the peculiar circumstances of the Deanery, the position is anything but an agreeable one." On the 5th of April 1850 old Daddy Woodard, who was parish clerk when Mr Markham came in 1838, and had held the post ever since, died of bronchitis. Charles Polley, a much younger man aged 35, was selected as his successor.

CHAPTER EIGHT

1850-1851

On the 11th of March 1850 David Markham had completed his fiftieth year. He was of commanding height, upwards of six feet, and proportionate width of chest; and his head was now bald, displaying a high and broad forehead. His handsome features were generally lighted up with a bright genial expression, especially when conversing with others; and they were even more striking in his graven moods. While his manner at once put people and children at their ease with him, from an instinct that he liked their company, he commanded the respect of all ages and ranks by his dignified courtesy, and their confidence by his firm yet conciliatory bearing. His influence was thus very great, and never greater than in the last three years of his life.

David Markham, after his return from Madeira, was at Nunappleton from the 29th of May to the 10th of June, where they were busily engaged in preparations for consecrating the church at Acaster, the new clergyman, Mr Hustler, having arrived. On the 4th, and all day of the 7th of June he was at the church with Lady Milner, and at Appleton arranging about Mr Hustler's house. He was much pleased with the church, though seeing some faults in the details, and he suggested many little things connected with the pulpit and communion table.

On June 10th he returned to Horkesley with his daughter Selina, who had now become very useful to him. His wife could not yet bear to go there, and remained at Nunappleton and Osberton until the Windsor residence began on the 24th of June.

His first duty was to commence his visitations as Rural Dean. On the 17th he visited the churches at Wormingford and Fordham, on the 18th Boxted, on the 20th West Bergholt, on the 21st Dedham and Langham, and on the 22nd Little Horkesley.

The Windsor residence was, in 1850, from the 1st of July to the 5th of September; and during that time many visits were received from relations and friends. David Markham also renewed his acquaintance with an old schoolfellow, Lord de Ros. "He is just as he was when I knew him 30 years ago." Lady and Miss Duncan came on the 15th of July for some days, afterwards Sir William Milner and Laura, and William Milner and his wife. Lord and Lady de Ros and their daughter also dined several times in the house in the cloisters, and went [on] excursions on the river with Selina and the Nevilles. Young George Egerton was at Eton and often came up to the cloisters to dinner. On the 7th of August "a picnic with the Nevilles, to Monkey Island – pulled an oar there, which I had not done for 20 years before, and found that I lost very little of my ancient skill." From the 21st to the 24th he and his daughter Selina were staying with the Keenes, at Swyncombe. On the 24th Mrs Baillie and her daughter May arrived at the cloisters, and staid until the 28th.

> It is very delightful to find the great affection that May has for us. In the afternoon of the 26th a *very interesting* drive with May and Fanny Baillie to Virginia Water. On the 27th much singing in the evening, May taking a part delightfully. The dear Bailies left us this morning (28th) and not without many tears.
>
> Buried poor old Captain Wragg, the Military Knight, this morning. He had expressed a wish that I should do it. The poor old man was so fond of my dear David.

During this residence he was very busily engaged in making arrangements for the chorister's school over the archway from the Horse-shoe cloisters, and in setting the course of instruction with Mr Pearson, the schoolmaster and Lay-clerk. On the 5th of September 1850 the family returned to Horkesley.

In his latter years David Markham paid special attention to archaeology, a study in which he had all his life taken great interest. Colchester, with its marvellous castle, its old walls, St. John's Gateway, St. Botolph's etc., offered an admirable field. All these remains had engaged his attention ever since he came to live in the neighbourhood. On the 12th of September 1850, in company with Mr Jenkins and Mr James Round, he had a grand exploration of the castle for three hours. Mr Jenkins had started a theory that Colchester Castle is the actual temple of Claudius. In this David Markham was unable to coincide, holding that it was obviously a Norman castle, though Roman materials were used in building it.

On September 25th Lady and Miss Duncan came to Horkesley, and Mr Calvert Jones from Gifford's Hall, who had also been at Malta. "We were a complete Malta party again, and only want of my poor David to make us very happy."

On the 4th of November 1850 David Markham went to Windsor for a commemoration service of the organist Mr Elvery; and also to see young George Egerton, who was ill at Eton.

> On the 5th, before chapel, I went to see Prince Albert about the music. He was very gracious, shook hands with me, and made me sit down, a rather unusual honor, and had a long chat. He signified his intention of coming to the afternoon service on Friday. On the 8th all went off well. It was a fine thing to see 100 Lay Clerks and boys file off before the chapter room, and still more to hear the first solemn and powerful union of voices in the confession.
>
> In the middle of the service I received a summons to come out on some very important business, and found Mrs George Milner in a carriage at the cloister door. She announced the deplorable intelligence of poor Caddy Carden having been shot dead by her husband's rifle, which was laid on the bench she was sitting on, and by accident fell, and in doing so was discharged, and the contents lodged in her brain.[85] We went down to Eton to break it

[85] Author's note quoted from the Diary of Henry Greville: Lady Carden was a charming woman and the idol of her family. She was the daughter of Sir William Milner and her mother was a Bentinck, a most amiable delightful lady whose attractions her daughter inherited. We heard this morning from William Milner from Templemore. Sir John Carden put the hammer of the rifle on the cap for safety, not being aware that of all things this is the least safe. The wind blew the gun down on its butt, and the vibration caused it to go off. The ball entered her ear and came out at the top of her head, so that her death was instantaneous. It is singular that only a few days before she had spoken to her sister-in-law of her death, as if she had some presentment that it was at hand, and gave very minute directions respecting her children (three little girls).and desiring that they might attend her funeral.

> to George Egerton, and then I went to Horkesley by the first train in hopes of getting there before Kate could know the deplorable event from the papers. She was as composed as possible under the circumstances, but looking wretched.

In November there was a long visit from Laura Markham, gone a week from Mr and Mrs Wickham. Willy Wickham had for years paid frequent visits at Horkesley, and he was always very welcome, being one of David Markham's favorite nephews. On the 1st of December Mrs Markham went to Nunappleton to meet Sir John Carden and his children – their first visit after the dreadful accident. She came back to London on the 17th, and her husband came up to meet her, going that evening to the Westminster Play with his old friends Sir David Dundas, Lord de Ros, and Mr Wickham. They stayed with Mr George Milner at 58 Caton Square, returning to Horkesley on the 19th. John and Henry Clements both passed their Christmas there. From January 5th to 27th, and February 21st to March 3rd 1851 David Markham suffered from severe attacks of gout.

On the 30th of January 1851 he went to his brother William at Ryde owing to the dangerous illness of his little niece Rose Markham. His god-child Mary died the day before of decline,[86] the same disease that had carried off poor Adela in 1848. On September 14th to 19th 1850 he had been up in London with his sister in law Mrs Markham, helping her when she came to consult doctors about poor Rose; and again on the 30th. He went to Ryde, arriving there on February 1st 1851, partly in the hopes of comforting the mourners on the death of his poor little godchild, and partly to see Rose.[87]

---

[86] Decline usually refers to a wasting disease where there is a gradual deterioration in the patient's condition, for example tuberculosis. Lesley Brown (Ed.), *The New Shorter Oxford English Dictionary*. Vol. 1. (Oxford: Clarendon Press, 1993) p.609.

[87] Author's note: A stained glass window was put up to the memory of Adela, Mary and Rose Markham, in Aberford Church, by their mother.

> Poor little Mary is to be buried in Binstead churchyard on Monday. I read the services at home to the family on Sunday, and walked in the afternoon with William and Edwin to see the grave. Afterwards read and conversed with Rose, who is very weak without a prospect of recovery. The funeral was at 11 of the 3rd, the church very prettily situated. Read to Rose, and she talked to me about her sister and her prospect of joining her.

For several days he remained at Ryde, reading and talking to his poor little niece; and had a touching conversation on taking leave of her, on the 9th of February. She died on the 18th of April and was also buried in Binstead church yard.

During April 1851 David Markham was busily engaged with [a] scheme for the establishment of a museum in Colchester Castle. On the 2nd he met Mr Charles Round, whose property it was, at the Board of Guardians, and obtained his consent to the appropriation of a part of the castle as a museum. The same day he called on Mr Brown, a farmer at Stanway, to examine his very complete collection of fossils of the Suffolk crag;[88] and he afterwards arranged with Mr James Round about a Committee to be formed, to carry out their schemes for forming a museum. He also framed rules, and set the work actively going, frequently in Colchester to consult about it.

In May 1851 was his second visitation as Rural Dean. On the 5th he went to Wivenhoe, Dedham, Langham, and Boxted. On the 6th to Wormingford, Fordham, Bergholt, and Little Horkesley. On the 9th he went with a party staying in the house, to show them the monuments in the Little Horkesley church.

On the 15th of May, to his great inconvenience, he was obliged to start for Dublin, at the urgent request of John Clements, to attend another trial. On arriving he found that the trial was on the day before, that he was not wanted, and had had his journey for nothing. After much conversation with Mr Murdoch on John's affairs, he got back to London on the 17th.

[88] Author's note: This collection was bequeathed, by Mr Brown, to the British Museum.

At this time there were many relations living in London, all or part of the year. His aunt Lady Mansfield was at Langham House, and all his sisters and their husbands had houses in London. Mr and Mrs Wickham lived at Chesterfield Street, Mr Stansfield being in Parliament,[89] had a house in Charles Street, and Colonel Mures,[90] also in Parliament, was in Curzon Street. Archdeacon and Mrs Bentinck were in Dean's Yard, Lady Elizabeth Clements at No. 2 Grosvenor Square, William Milner,[91] also in Parliament, in Eaton Place, and Mr George Milner at 58 Eaton Square. David Markham, when in London, generally slept either in Charles Street or Eaton Square. On the 19th of May 1851 he spent the whole day, seven hours, in the Crystal Palace in Hyde Park "and was much charmed with this enchanting sight of fairy land." He was with his daughter Selina. Next day he went again with Mr Stansfield, chiefly occupied with the very beautiful things in the French Department, and spending a good deal of time among the machinery. On the 22nd he was again there all day, with his sister in law Mrs Markham, returning to Horkesley on the 24th. He frequently visited the Exhibition during the summer, always with much enjoyment.

On the 26th, and again on the 27th, he induced his wife to walk with him round the glebe at Horkesley, an exertion which she had not been able to attempt for many months, and her ability to make it gave him great pleasure. She took the same walk again on the 28th and 30th. His younger daughters were now becoming agreeable companions, and on the 3rd of June he went on a botanising expedition with Gena to Pitchberry wood.

The Windsor residence, in 1851, was from June 25th to August 29th. Young George Egerton and Granville Leveson Gower were constantly up from Eton. Mr and Mrs Milner, and their daughter Edith, also came to stay; and on July 9th to 14th young John Markham, "a fine handsome lad of 16." On the 12th his uncle took him to the Crystal Palace. Owing to its being the year

89 Author's note: M.P. for Haddersfield.

90 Author's note: M.P. for Renfrewshire.

91 Author's note: M.P. for York.

of the Great Exhibition, there was an unusual number of visits from relations and friends at the cloisters. On July 21st Mr Markham was nominated Precentor.[92]

Mr Baker, who had been Curate at Horkesely since 1844 was presented by the Dean and Chapter of Windsor with the living of Monklands, in Herefordshire which, after much hesitation, he accepted in August 1851;[93] and on the 24th of September, the Reverend H.W. Edwards,[94] the new Curate, took his place at Horkesley. Mr Baker preached his last sermon on the 5th of October, on the 6th the children and parishioners took leave of him in the Infant School, and he left on the morning of the 11th.

The family left Windsor on the 29th of August 1851, and went to Cowes to be with Colonel Markham and his family. On the 30th David Markham went on board the famous Yankee yacht *America*; and on the 1st of September to Binsted to see the grave stone over Mary and Rose Markham.

Colonel Markham had a schooner yacht at Cowes, the *Merlin*, and on the 2nd of September he and David Markham sailed in her, to pay a visit to their brother John and his family, who then lived at Guernsey. They left Cowes at 2. P.M., and anchored in St. Peter's Port at 10 next morning.

> We arrived at Roncesvalles (the name of their brother's house) at 2 o'clock, and after luncheon walked with Jack to the grand harbour. After dinner we went back to the *Merlin*, and slept on

[92] The term Precentor may describe a person who directs singing in a choir, a minor Canon or chaplain, or, in a cathedral of the Old Foundation, a member of a chapter ranking next below the Dean. Lesley Brown (Ed.), *The New Shorter Oxford English Dictionary*. Vol. 2. (Oxford: Clarendon Press, 1993) p.2324. Based upon David Markham's status within the Church of England and his long standing as a Canon of Windsor it is assumed that he was being honoured with a rank just below the Dean of the Chapter.

[93] Author's note: The Vicar of Monklands succeeded his Father as third Baronet on November 2nd 1859. He named his vicarage at Monklands, which he built himself, Horkesley House. Sir Henry Baker died at Monklands on February 12th 1877.

[94] Author's note: In 1854 he married Miss Bonnor, the Governess at Horkesley, and has a large family. 1853 Vicar of Orleton in Herefordshire. (worth £156. pop. 591).

> board. On the 4th they drove to a very pretty little cove about 4 miles from St. Peter's Port, called Moulin de Huettes. It is almost surrounded by rocks of very picturesque forms, and worth seeing.

During this visit to Guernsey David Markham made the acquaintance of his nephew George, and [the] Markham's went over to Portsmouth to see the colours trooped and hear the band play. Every day there was a cruise in the *Merlin*; and after a pleasant visit of a fortnight at Cowes, David Markham, with his wife and daughter Selina, went thence to pay a visit to Lady Elizabeth Clements at Long Ditton on the 12th, staying until the 17th. On the 16th Mr Markham, with his daughters Selina and Gena, "went to the Royal Gardens at Kew: much interested in every department, but it would take days to see it properly." The family returned to Horkesley on the 17th of September 1851.

Chapter Nine

1851-1852

The Arctic Expedition returned to England in the autumn of 1851, and on the 2nd of October Clements Markham arrived at Horkesley.

> He is looking handsome and well, and in excellent spirits, and not one jot the worse for all his hardships. But he talks seriously of leaving the navy. October 3rd spent the whole day at home with our dear boy. His accounts of the dreary winter and exploring expeditions were very interesting.

From the 4th to the 9th he was at Woolwich while the ships were being paid off, his Father coming on board the *Assistance* on the 7th; and on the 18th to the 24th his Arctic messmate R. Vesey Hamilton visited at Horkesley. On the 1st of November, Captain Quin, an old shipmate in the *Collingwood*, arrived on a visit at Horkesley, staying until the 4th, "a nice agreeable little man."

The wish of his son to leave the navy was a great disappointment to David Markham; but he consented, only urging that he would not do so before he had passed his examination for Lieutenant. Some of his log books had been stolen while the *Assistance* was paying off at Woolwich, and his Father worked for hours, often late into the night, ruling and writing the headings of the columns for the new logs. On December 1st he went down to Portsmouth, and returned home on Christmas day, having passed on board the *Excellent* the day before. It was at first intended that he should take his degree at Oxford. He worked up his classics with Mr Edwards, the Curate at Horkesley, for his matriculation; and on December 12th his Father went to Oxford and arranged for his being received at St. Mary Hall; but it was afterwards decided that the loss of time involved in going to Oxford would be undesirable, and that he should at once begin to read for the law.

Meanwhile David Markham with his wife, his son Clements and daughter Selina, paid some visits in Yorkshire. They were first at Nunappleton from the 7th to the 17th of November 1851. The new church of Acaster had been consecrated, and on the 8th David Markham, with his son and his sister in law Laura Milner, walked to see it, and was much pleased with the memorial window to his dear son David, which he saw in its place for the first time. On Sunday the 9th, at the afternoon service, he preached in Acaster church, taking for his text the words in Genesis (XXVIII.16.17) "And Jacob awaked out of his sleep and he said, Surely the Lord is in this place."

Towards the end of a very beautiful sermon he said,

> It is impossible to look around these walls without reflecting on what this spot was but a few short months ago. Then one, wearied and way worn like Jacob, wandering to this place might, when overcome by sleep, and resting his head on the green turf, have been awakened by the same consciousness of dread at feeling himself in the sight of God. But imagine the same man suddenly roused from his slumber and finding reared over his head a beautiful tabernacle (such as this in which we are now assembled) with every provision for the service of God. Were he suddenly to become aware that such an unexpected event had really occurred, and that the Almighty had put it into the heart of one kind friend to effect all this; would he not be almost mute with astonishment, and when he had the power to utter would he not be inclined to pour out his heart in grateful acknowledgement, and feel more strongly than ever that 'God indeed was in this place.' Let me entreat you then, as one in whom many of you, I believe, once confided, to listen to a word in season, and never to allow yourselves to cross the threshold of this holy place without considering unto whose presence you are about to come. There are many here who recognize in me one whose ministrations I humbly hope they once valued; who have often kindly taken advice, and occasionally reproof from my lips; there are many who were infants when I was called to a more distant sphere of action, and who have now grown to man's estate, and to whom my name is all that is familiar to them; and there are some too who, from the natural changes that time produces, are perfect strangers to me. But I am sure there are none who will not take in good part a few words of advice from one who has, for nearly a

> quarter of a century, been deeply interested in the spiritual welfare of this parish. I, therefore, seize this opportunity of saying a few words to my old parishioners and those who have succeeded some of them, in allusion to the subject we have been considering.

His concluding words were an exhortation to a pure life, and to a practical appreciation and use of the benefits that had been conferred on them. During his stay at Nunappleton he was chiefly engaged in settling matters at Acaster with Lady Milner, and in staking out a new road across the park to Acaster for her.

From Nunappleton he went, with his family, to visit Lord and Lady Wenloch at Escrick, on the 17th and 18th November. He walked to Escrick, with his son, passing through Stillingfleet on the way, and calling at many cottages. This was David Markham's last visit to his old parish.

On the 19th they went from Escrick to Harewood, to visit David Markham's old friends Lord and Lady Harewood. Here there was a large party, and three days were very agreeably spent. The visit at Becca was from the 22nd to the 29th of November, and at Esholt from the 29th of November to the 5th of December, after which they returned to Nunappleton. Colonel Markham's health was in a most precarious state, and gave reason for the gravest anxiety. But he was still able to go about, he read a good deal, and took great interest in everything that was passing round him; while his affection for his brother, and pleasure at seeing him, never waned.

David Markham was at Nunappleton again from the 5th to the 9th of December. On the 6th he walked over to Kelfield by Wharfe-mouth, to visit Mrs Buckle and all his old friends. It was for the last time. The people of Kelfield and Stillingfleet felt a warm friendship for him. He never missed an opportunity of visiting them whenever he was in Yorkshire, and these periodical greetings of their old pastor were a source of unmixed pleasure to the villagers.[95]

[95] Author's note: Old Mrs Buckle of Kelfield died on the 2nd of March 1853, only 28 days before David Markham. Her last wish was that her old pastor should have her black letter Cramner Bible of 1541; which on her death, was sent over to Nunappleton by her niece.

On the 9th he took Fred Egerton down to Portsmouth to pass for a Naval Cadet, and put up at the *Fountain* in High Street, to be with his son Clements, who was passing out in gunnery. The next two days were passed in great anxiety lest Fred should fail in his examination; but on the 11th Captain Chads announced that he had got through, and, having obtained for him a month's leave, his uncle adjourned for luncheon on board the *Excellent* with his son. On the 12th he was at Oxford, and on the 13th he returned to Horkesley.

But there continued to be serious cause of alarm on account of the state of his brother's health, and on the 15th of January 1852 he again went to Becca to see him.

> I found William very cheerful, and looking much as I had left him six weeks before. On the 16th I walked with him about the place, and had long conversations with poor Lucy on many subjects. Dr. Ellerton does not seem to think that poor William can last more than four months, even if he is not carried off by some sudden attack. On Sunday the 18th I staid at home to read prayers with William.

On the 20th David Markham saw his brother for the last time. "A sad leave taking altogether." He returned to Horkesley, but on the 27th he was again summoned to Becca, arriving there on the 28th. Colonel Markham had died suddenly at last, on Monday the 26th. David found his sister Emma at Becca, and his nephew William, with whom, and the old steward George King, he was much occupied for several days.

> On Monday the 2nd of February my poor brother's remains were consigned to the grave at Aberford. All the neighbourhood had arrived in good time. The pall bearers were his old friends, Lord Harewood, Arthur and Edwin Lascelles, Mr Fairfax of Newton Kyme, Mr Edward York of Wighill, Mr Wharton of Aberford and Mr Fox of Branham. Most of the people in Aberford were standing at their doors, and I observed the greater part of the women were crying. I read a service for the mourners after we came back from Aberford.

In the following days he had much executorship business, and returned to Horkesley on the 7th of February. Colonel Markham was only in his 56th year. His loss was much felt in his own neighbourhood, where he was beloved and respected.[96]

On the 23rd of March David Markham went to Becca again to help his sister-in-law and nephew in their arrangements, and he was at work all day, on the 24th, at executorship accounts. His sister in law Mrs Egerton drove over from Thorp arch on the 25th to consult him on various matters; and he was again fully occupied on the 26th. This was his last visit to Becca, his birthplace, and the home of his childhood and youth.

On the 27th he went to Nunappleton; and on Sunday the 28th he performed both services at Acaster church. This was his last visit to Nunappleton. He returned to Horkesley on the 30th of March 1852.

David Markham, during these later years, had devoted much of his leisure time to literary pursuits, independently of his acquisition of the Italian, and afterwards of the Hebrew language. He allowed himself £20 a year for the purchase of books and engravings, of which he had a fine collection, including several by Hollar.[97] One source of interest and amusement was the collection of a series of prints and autographs of celebrated old Westminsters; which became very extensive in course of time and was arranged with reference to the different reigns from Elizabeth, each commencing with engravings and autographs of the Sovereigns and the Head Masters.[98]

[96] Author's note: A stained glass window was put up to his memory, in Aberford Church, at the end of the south aisle; by his son.

[97] Author's note: He had bound up in a volume, XXVI plates of the life of Christ by Albert Durer, for which he printed the title page. The portrait of Durer is by Hollar 1645. A Virgin and Child is by Durer himself 1514. The rest are fine copies of Durer's engravings, probably by Hollar.

[98] Author's note: This interesting collection was presented, by his son, to the Elizabethan Club of Old Westminsters, where it was highly appreciated. Extract from the Report of the Committee of the Elizabethan Club of the Wesminsters for 1873: The Committee take this opportunity of acknowledging the handsome present of a valuable collection of prints and autographs of numerous old Westminsters made to the Club by Mr Clements R. Markham, and of recording their thanks to him for the gift.

Among his pictures was a good Sir Godfrey Knallen of a Bowles ancestor given to him in 1851; a fine portrait of Lady Milner, his wife's grandmother, by Sir Thomas Lawrence; a portrait of a gentleman of the 17th century by Walker; landscaspes by Sir George Beaumont and Mr Oldfield Bowles; some good sea pieces; an exquisite portrait of a Monk on panel by a Dutch painter;[99] a copy of the worshipping of the Magi by Rubens, at Brussels; a Zuccarelli; and water colours by Carter, Nesfield, and Schrantz not framed.

His library occupied two rooms. The works on law, divinity and, theology were in his study, while in the cheerful library and morning room were the collection of works on history, topography, geography and travel, poetry, biography, and books of reference. His antiquarian studies were now chiefly in the direction of local and especially Colchester archaeology. He also, in the spring of 1852, collected together and put in order his materials respecting the Markham family, which he had commenced more than twenty years before. He brought the whole into a narrative form arranged in four sections, devoted to the four branches of Cotham, Becca, Allerton, and Sedgebrook, with appendices. In tracing out the history of the family the cadets of which had, on many occasions, been connected with important events in the general history of the country, many things were brought to light and treated of which possessed general interest and the work, thus nearly completed by David Markham, was of considerable historical and antiquarian value. Among other points of history, fresh evidence was adduced as to the identity of the judge who committed Prince Henry for contempt; and with regard to the recusants of Queen Elizabeth's time.

Among the documents collected by David Markham, the most important were a pedigree and a manuscript purchased at the sale at Leeds Castle in 1840. The pedigree is that of Sir Griffin Markham, who was associated with Sir Walter Raleigh in the alleged plot to place Arabella Stuart on the throne, in 1603. It is 11 feet 10 inches long, 2 feet 8 inches wide, on four skins of parchment. The emblazoned shields of arms are 155 in number. The latest date on it

99 Author's note: Gerard Dow.

is 1617, and it is attested by the autograph signature of John Camden, Clarenceux king of Arms, who died in 1623. So that the pedigree, which is in excellent preservation, must have been drawn up between those two dates. The manuscript volume consists of 18 leaves folio, in the handwriting of Francis Markham, a cousin and contemporary of Sir Griffin. Besides a glossary of Anglo Saxon words, and lists of names of persons and places with their derivations, it consists of a history of the Markham Family dated July 27th 1601. In this history it is distinctly stated that Sir John Markham was the judge who committed Prince Henry to the Fleet Prison for contempt of court. The volume concludes with an autobiography of Francis Markham, which furnishes an interesting sketch of the life of a cadet of good family at the close of the sixteenth century.[100]

David Markham also collected most of the rare works of the sixteenth century by Gervase and Francis Markham including a quaint manuscript called "The Horse Marshall" which he transcribed; and a copy of Thomas a Kempis belonging to Gervase Markham, with probably one of the earliest specimens of a book plate, in the beginning.

David Markham was also much interested, during 1852, in matters relating to Arctic research, and especially in the proceedings of the expedition which had returned in the previous autumn. His son was engaged to give a lecture at the Literary Institute at Colchester on the 18th of February, and David Markham was busily employed for several days, preparing large scale diagram maps, and painting six exceedingly clever water colour sketches of Arctic scenes. By special request the lecture was delivered again on the 31st of March, when David Markham took the chair; and his son's old Arctic Messmate, R. Vesey Hamilton was present. "The lecture went off excellently well and seemed to afford universal satisfaction." His son also wrote a little volume containing a history of the Arctic Expedition of 1850-51, called *Franklin's Footsteps*

[100] Author's note: See an account of the Pedigree of Sir Griffin Markham, and of Francis Markham's History of his Family, in the number of the *Proceedings of the Society of Antiquaries* for November 17th 1859.

which was published by Chapman and Hall, and was a success. But this was due to David Markham's editorial supervision, and to the form into which he eventually brought it, by judicious excisions and corrections.

From the 8th to the 12th of February 1852 his nephew young John Markham was at Horkesley, having received an appointment as Student Interpreter in China, from Lord Malmesbury;[101] and from the 3rd to the 8th of March another nephew, James Mure, was paying a visit there. His mother Mrs Mure, with her daughter Emma, were at Horkesley from the 6th to the 14th of May.

Selina Markham had met Captain Quin several times in London, and his visit to Horkesley enabled them to become more intimate. "March 8th Selina and I went into the parish. During our walk we had a long talk on what took place in London. She seems to like Captain Quin, and he appears to be devoted to her. Kate has written to ask him here. I trust it will all turn out for dear Iny's happiness." Captain Quin arrived on the 13th of March and, after obtaining permission, he proposed and was accepted on Monday the 15th. He stated that his income was £1040 a year, and that on his Father's death he would succeed to his Irish property. "I trust there is every prospect of happiness in this union. All his family are prepared to receive Selina most cordially; but she will be a sad loss to our fire side."

Richard Robert Quin was born on August 23rd 1820, and entered the navy in 1834. He served in the first war in China, and became a Lieutenant in 1841.[102] From 1842 to 1844 he was in the

---

[101] Author's note: John Markham was born at Leghorn on April 1st 1835. He went out to China in 1852, and served at Canton, Foochow, and Hong Kong until 1857; when he was appointed First Assistant at Bangkok. On February 16th 1858 he married Miss Caroline Rickett at Hong Kong, and had two daughters, Marianne born in 1861, and Florence in 1865. In 1858 John Markham became Vice Consul at Shanghae; and Consul at Chefu in 1868. He died at Shanghae on October 9th 1871. "He was an able and energetic Consul, a courteous and kindly chief, a most popular and genial man."

[102] The First China War referred to is the First Opium War, 1839-1842. For more on this conflict see, Jack Gray, *Rebellions and Revolutions: China from the 1800s to 2000*, 2nd Edition. (Oxford: Oxford University Press, 2002) pp. 39-48; and, W. Travis Hanes and Frank Sanello, *The Opium Wars*, (Illinois: Sourcebooks Inc., 2002).

Belvidere in the Mediterranean, when he was a messmate of Alfred Ryder, and they continued through life to be intimate friends. In 1844 he joined the *Collingwood*, when he was shipmate with his future brother-in-law Clements Markham. He became a Commander in 1846, commanded the brig *Water Witch* on the coast from 1848 to 1851, and was posted in February 1852.

Richard Quin was the only surviving son of Lord George Quin (the second son of the Marquis of Headford) by Lady Georgiana Spencer. His only sister Lavinia was married to Mr Watson of Rockingham Castle.

There were many letters of congratulation on this engagement: "one from Lady Cowper which gave me much pleasure from allusions to former happy days at Newby. On the 15th of April Lord George Quin came to Horkesley, and paid a very satisfactory visit."

The wedding was fixed for the 1st of June 1852. On May 31st there arrived Lord George Quin, Mr and Mrs Wickham, Archdeacon Bentinck, Henry Milner, Frank Fogiambe, Willy Wickham, Willy Markham, and Mr and Mrs Watson.

> Archdeacon Bentinck performed the ceremony and the wedding went off as well as possible, all working to make it do so. The arrangements for going to church through arbours of flowers were quite beautiful, and the breakfast was a great success. They went by a special train to Rockingham Castle.

The bells of Horkesley rang merrily, but not of Horkesley only. Old Slater, the Sexton, and the other bellringers of Stillingfleet also sent forth merry peels on the 1st of June, in honour of the marriage of their old pastor's daughter.

Selina was the life of the house, and her absence was sorely felt. Her father wrote, on June 2nd, "Nothing can equal the desolate state the house seems to be [in]." Aunt Lady Mansfield, and her daughters Lady Elizabeth and Lady Georgina Murray were at Horkesley from the 18th to the 21st of June. The Windsor residence, in 1852, was from the 24th of June to the 30th of August.

David Markham was, this year, a good deal engaged with improvements in the old Windsor Chapter room, in which he took great interest. The Quins arrived from Hagley (Lord Lyttleton's) on the 7th of July, and staid until the 11th of August, when they set out for a tour in the north of Italy. There were also visits from Mrs Milner, with her baby,[103] for several days, Lord Carlisle, Colonel and Mrs Stuart, and Mr and Mrs Bowen who had been so kind to poor David at Madeira. Young George Egerton and Granville Leveson Gower were often at the cloisters, and on July 14th there was a large dinner party of Eton boys, sons of old Yorkshire friends – George Egerton, Walter Lascelles, George and Dick Fox, Ferdy Fairfax, and two Cloughs. They all played at the racing game.

"July 1st – Clym divulged to me his anxious wish to go to South America. I am much averse to this scheme for many reasons. It is a sad unsettling business this taste for writing, and I fear will turn out most unprofitable." Yet he gave his consent, put aside £500 for the expenses, and never allowed any foreboding as to the result to appear, by word or look. There was nothing but indulgent kindness to his son, and a warm interest in the objects of the proposed expedition.[104]

> August 12th – we are all very busy about Clym's Peruvian tour, getting letters and preparing outfit. August 20th – I hope that the scheme will turn out better than at first sight it seemed likely to do, but it is a long lonely business, and I have not much heart about it. He left us at 2:20 P.M. today."

---

[103] Author's note: Granville Milner born December 28th 1851.

[104] Clements Markham's Peruvian expedition would prove a turning point in his career and launch him on the path of becoming a respected explorer/geographer and writer. He spent 1852-53 in Peru exploring Inca sites and the Incan language, Quechua. He would return to Peru in 1860 when he was commissioned to collect seeds of the Cinchona tree, a source of quinine, to be transported and planted to India and therefore making quinine available there. He would later to travel to India, Abyssinia, and Greenland, and publish accounts of his travels. See, Elizabeth Baigent, "Sir Clements Robert Markham" *Oxford Dictionary of National Biography*. (Oxford: Oxford University Press, 2004) Online Ed. For a selected list of Sir Clements Markham's publications see Appendix Twenty: Select Publications of Sir Clements R. Markahm.

In his letters to his son in Peru, he wrote more cheerfully, urging him to accuracy in his plans and measurements, and making many useful suggestions with reference to his investigations; but looking forward anxiously to his return home as soon as possible. That 20th of August 1852 was, alas! The last time David Markham was ever destined to see his surviving son. He parted with him reluctantly and almost with a foreboding that it would be a final separation.

CHAPTER TEN

MINISTRATIONS AT GREAT HORKESLEY (1838-1853)

As David Markham advanced in years, there was a progressive modification of his opinions on several points, which showed itself in his ministration. But his toleration for the views of others, his never failing charitableness were always the same; and in their exercise lay the secret of the great influence he had over people of all classes with whom he was brought in contact. He was most indulgent to the weaknesses of others, yet he never spared himself, and while the working of his generous catholic mind appeared in his kindly tolerance, he maintained the great principles of his own creed with uncompromising firmness.

The tendency of his mind, as his years increased, was towards a stricter and more exact observance of the duties of his holy calling, both as regards the secular care of the people entrusted to him, and the performance of the services of the church.

At Stillingfleet he visited his people very constantly, and was their intimate friend as well as their pastor. But at Horkesley he brought the duty of visitation, with the efficient aid of his curate, to a regular system, by which a thorough sympathy was established between the clergy and the people. One part of his system was to have a *visiting cycle* so as to ensure that no family was overlooked.[105] In 1851 the population of the parish of Great Horkesley was 747, consisting of 165 families, inhabiting 164 houses. Of these families 132 were engaged in agriculture and 29 in trade.[106]

---

[105] See Appendix Twelve, *The Visitation Cycle.*

[106] Author's Note: In 1861 the population was 769, and the number of inhabited houses 172. In 1871 the population was 844 (males 419 and females 425) and the number of inhabited houses 177.

The old benefit clubs held at public houses, and founded on the most insecure basis, were very unsatisfactory; and in 1836 the Stoke and Melford Mutual Benefit Association was established. As this club was well managed, David Markham encouraged the young people of Great Horkesley to join it, and always took an active part in its management. When he came, in 1838, there were 11 members in the parish, while in 1848 there were 60.

There were not many special benefactions in the parish. The principal one, called the *Elmstead Charity*, consisted of lands left by John Guyou, by his will dated 5th April 1509, for the relief and maintenance of honest poor born in the parish, or who had dwelt in it for three years; to be disposed of by the Rector, Churchwardens, and four of the chief inhabitants. The funds of this Charity, which amounted to £33 a year, had been very improperly devoted to the purposes of the poor rate. David Markham objected to this, and it was arranged that 7 poor persons should receive a shilling each weekly, and that the remainder should be devoted to building poor boys as apprentices. In 1841, as very few persons applied for money for apprenticeships, three more weekly recipients of a shilling were added, making the number ten, afterwards increased to eleven.

The erection of the Infant School, combined with the National School, placed the education of the parish on a thoroughly efficient footing. The number of the children at the former was 55, and at the latter 50. David Markham always took special interest in the schools, constantly teaching himself, and keeping up a careful supervision. He was very fond of children, which they knew almost by an instinct, and his favourite walk, up to the last month of his life, was to the Infant School.

But it was one of his most anxious aims to devise means whereby some sort of education should be continued in after life. He established a lending library which was kept in the vestry, and which eventually consisted of 300 carefully selected volumes; the books being issued and returned after evening service on Sundays.[107]

[107] Author's Note: The lending library was given up by his successors, and the books were left unused in the vestry. In 1878 Mr Storr utilized many of them, in forming the library for the Horkesley Club.

He also established a Club for the purchase of books, which enabled the poor, by small deposits, to make useful purchases at the end of the year. In 1843 he made an attempt to establish an adult school after working hours, for young men to obtain some rudimentary instruction. It lasted for a little while, but in a few months dwindled almost to nothing and was given up. In 1848 he thought that a more favourable result might be obtained by using the infant school in the centre of the parish, instead of the national school at the end of it. He drew up a scheme with a view to combining the instruction of young men with a reading society for those of advanced age. The first meeting took place on the 13th of November 1848, when 15 young men became members, and the meetings continued to be held twice a week. David Markham also established weekly cottage lectures, which were held on Wednesdays at noon, in a house belonging to Mr. Sadler. The object was to explain portions of scripture to the old and infirm, for whom it was difficult or impossible to go so far as to church. These lectures continued to be well attended, and were productive of much good. The Rector continued to be Guardian of the poor, from 1843 until his death, constantly attending at Board, and discharging the duties actively and zealously.

The results of David Markham's purely spiritual ministrations were as clearly marked as was the improvement of the people under his charge in all other respects. When he came there were 66 communicants,[108] and the sacrament was administered 6 times in the year. At the time of his death there were 18 administrations, and the number of communicants had increased to 140.[109] Besides

---

[108] Those receiving Holy Communion, especially regularly. Lesley Brown (Ed.), *The New Shorter Oxford English Dictionary*. Vol. 1. (Oxford: Clarendon Press, 1993) p. 454.

[109] Author's Note: There was a dissenter named John Green who, in Dr Ward's time, had built himself a pretentious house by the road side, at the Colchester end of the parish, which he called 'Terrace Hall'. He also built a dissenting chapel. In 1851 his son and four daughters voluntarily came to Mr Markham for instruction, expressing a wish to be received into the Church of England. Mr Markham took great interest in them. The girls received adult baptism on Feb. 24th 1851. Amelia (born 18290 was aged 22, Adelaide (born 1831) aged 20, Charlotte (born 1834) aged 17, and Charlotte (born 1836) aged 15. The father,

the two sermons on Sunday, there was a morning service on every Saint's day, when a lecture was delivered on the life and acts of the Saint; and, besides persons from the Rectory, there was generally a congregation of 8 or 10 parishioners. David Markham rightly felt that these services were proper in themselves, while they might often prove a comfort to those who were able to attend them: and this was so.

His sermons on special occasions, and especially when he advocated the cause of some useful society or charity, were, apart from their earnest eloquence, both interesting and instructive. In his periodical discourses on missionary work, with special reference to the Society for the Propagation of the Gospel, he secured the attention of his audience by the interest he gave to their proceedings. At one time he explained the history of the operations of the Society from its commencement, at others he gave accounts of special work in China, Southern India, and other parts. In these missionary sermons, when preached in other churches, he always urged the desirability of forming parochial associations such as were so successful at Horkesley, meeting once a quarter.

> Those interested in missionary proceedings should meet occasionally and communicate freely on the subject, get together all the information within their reach, become acquainted with the wants of their fellow creatures in distant lands, and by thus encouraging each other, and exciting one another's zeal, neighbours will catch the same feeling, and each parish will then become a nucleus for the support of the Society.

In 1850, at the time of the Papal Aggression, David Markham preached four sermons evincing much research and sound learning, but at the same time clear and never rising above the capacity of a country congregation. The first was introductory, when he took for his text *I Thessalonians V. 21*, "Prove all things, hold fast that which is good." The second was on Papal Supremacy, and, as appears from a memorandum, he had studied the Apostolic

John Layzell Green, died in 1864 aged 68, and was buried under a pretentious disfiguring tomb in the S.E. corner of the churchyard.

Constitutions, the Councils of Nice Antioch and Constantinople, St. Cyprian, St. Gregory, St. Jerome, and Bingham's works, in its preparation. The two others were on transubstantiation and other Popish errors. These sermons were preached on the 1st, 8th, 15th, and 22nd of December 1850.

His sermons on the festivals of the church, and on confirmation, baptism, and the holy communion show that his views were those of a sound churchman, free from extreme sacerdotalism on the one hand, and from what is called evangelicalism on the other. Yet they are very clear and precise, and as exhortations are earnest and eloquent. But his discourses on moral duties and on the necessary virtues that a Christian must cultivate, were perhaps the most striking and had the most abiding effect on the minds of those who heard them. He, on several occasions, received letters from strangers who had formed part of his audience, expressing their thanks for the good effect upon their minds of what they had heard; and other persons, besides Queen Adelaide, begged to be allowed to have copies of particular sermons.

The last time he was able to perform divine service in church was on the 13th of March 1853, 18 days before his death. He preached in the morning, and the subject of his sermon was 'Prayer', taking his text from the epistle of Jude (part of the 20th verse) "Praying in the Holy Ghost." He explained that prayer was an art which, like other arts, must be learnt; that, although it must be spontaneous and spring from the heart, still it must be properly directed and skilfully managed; and that the most clear and unerring instructor was the holy scriptures. He then enumerated the various passages in which prayer is referred to, with a short commentary on each.

> Every motive of interest, every feeling of gratitude and love, should excite us to unceasing prayer to Him who alone can answer it. In your stated times of daily prayer, and in the numerous avocations which will not allow of formal prayer, cultivate, depend upon, and use the assistance of the Holy Ghost. Let your visits to God's footstool be with the intent to know and enjoy more of his unspeakable love, praying by and for the Holy Spirit,

> to be 'preserved in his love', and thus wait for the mercy of our Lord Jesus Christ unto eternal life.

These were the last public words of David Markham in his ministration of Great Horkesley; a faithful, zealous and untiring ministration of fifteen years. He was called away, in the midst of a useful career, ready and prepared to go, but alas! There has been none to fill his place.

CHAPTER ELEVEN

USEFULNESS AND ACTIVITY OF HIS LAST MONTHS

David Markham was never more zealously active in all his duties, more helpful to others, and his usefulness was never more generally felt than during the last few months of his life. It seemed as if the difficulty of replacing him, the irremediable character of his loss increased as the end drew nearer.

The departure of his son for South America was a source of anxiety and of foreboding. On the 21st of August he wrote "Very melancholy. The house apparently deserted. Only Kate and I at dinner."

On the 4th of August he stood Godfather for little Constance Seymour,[110] his cousin Emily's eighth child, at the chapel in the park, Lady Charles Fitz Roy and Mrs Bruce being Godmothers. During his residence of 1852 he saw a good deal of his Aunt Lady Mansfield and her daughters, and of the Nevilles.

On August 31st David Markham, with his wife and two younger daughters, Gena and Gertrude, left Windsor and set out for Burlington where they intended to stay for a month. They travelled with Mrs Baillie and her daughters as far as Peterborough, and this was the last time David Markham was destined to see his favourite cousins. He visited the cathedral, and then went with his daughter Gena to visit Thorp, where he had been with a private tutor when a boy. On September 1st they went on to Burlington, and took a house for a month. Mrs. Markham and her children, Mr Foljambe and Lady Milton, and William and Georgina Milner with their children were also there. David Markham took many

110 Author's Note: lady Constance Seymour was born on July 9th 1852. On Nov. 2nd 1871 she married Colonel St. John Borne of Sotterly Park in Suffolk.

long walks with his daughter Gena on the sands, and often sat with Mr Foljambe. On the 8th they all made a sketching expedition to Flamborough Head; on the 13th David Markham drove with his sister in law, Mrs Markham, to Brevton Agnes; on the 16th to dane's Dyke; on the 17th to Filey; on the 22nd to Thornwick Bay; and on the 24th, with Gena, to Scarborough, and afterwards to see Boynton, Sir George Strickland's deserted old house. "On the 29th Gena and I took a last look of Burlington Harbour from the south pier."

They left Burlington on the 30th of September, slept at Peterborough, and returned to Horkesley on the 1st of October 1852. On the 12th the Quins arrived from a tour in the north of Italy.

During the following months David Markham was very hard at work in his parish, visiting and teaching at the schools; and he was also more than usually engaged in useful work at Colchester. On the 21st of October he was at a Provisional Committee, of which he was a leading member, for establishing a County Antiquarian Society. On November 9th he attended the Committee for Church and School Building at Colchester. On December 13th he was at another Provisional Committee Meeting to arrange details, and on the 14th at a large meeting when the County Archaeological Society was established. The moving of the resolution for founding a Museum was entrusted to him, and before the business commenced he had names down for £160. "Dined at the 'Cups' with thirty other archaeologists, retiring with Gordon Rebow to James Round's for tea." On the 22nd he attended a Committee Meeting of the new Essex Archaeological Society. While engaged in the formation of this Society David Markham was thrown into very pleasant relations with Dr Duncan who was then practicing at Colchester, and has since attained eminence as a man of science.[111] On the 31st he was at

[111] Author's Note: Dr Duncan became an eminent geologist, especially as regards coral formations; professor at the Cooper's Hill Engineering College, and President of the Geological Society. Born in 1824 Professor Peter Martin Duncan died 28 May 1891. He practiced at Colchester from about 1850 to 1860, and was Mayor.

another E.A.S. Society Meeting, again on the 5th of January 1853, on the 15th, and on February 2nd when he was occupied for a long time with Dr Duncan, arranging plans for the new Museum. On the 17th of February he again attended an E.A.S. Meeting and on the 25th a Church Building Committee at Chelmsford. On the 9th and 16th of March he was again at Colchester at an E.A.S. Committee Meeting; and on the 17th he went to Chelmsford to be present at a meeting of the Council of the Essex Archaeological Society. He was mainly instrumental in forming this useful institution, and was most indefatigable in the work of its organization.

During this period there was a succession of visitors at Horkesley. From the 18th to the 20th of October he had a visit from young Prescott, son of the Historian, who had been very kind to his son Clements in America.[112] From the 19th to the 28th the two Miss Nevilles (twins) were there, and Mr baker came from the 26th to the 10th of November. But from November 2nd to 6th David Markham was obliged to be at Windsor for a chapter, dining with his aunt Lady Mansfield at Lovel Hill on the 2nd, with Mr Cust on the 3rd, and the Deanery on the two other days. On the 6th he went to see Frank and Alfred Markham at Westminster, the latter entering the navy on the 9th of November, and joining the *Agamemnon*. On the 22nd Mrs Egerton and her two little girls, Mary and Lucy, arrived at Horkesley and staid until the 2nd of December. On the 23rd Mr Seymour Neville came, staying until the 29th. From December 9th to 11th David Markham paid a visit to Archdeacon Burney at Wickham Bishops; and from the 27th to the 29th he and his wife were staying at Danbury with the Bishop of Rochester and Lady Sarah Murray; where there was a large party. "Kate seems to enjoy herself. She is always better

[112] The author is referring to the famous American historian William H. Prescott, best known for his *History of the Conquest of Mexico* (1843), and *Conquest of Peru* (1847). Clements Markham would no doubt have benefited from meeting such a scholar on Peru and remained an admirer of his work. Peter Blanchard writes that "While stuck in the ice during the winter of 1850-51 he re-read William Hickling Prescott's classic history of the conquest of Peru so that he knew it 'almost by heart.'" Peter Blanchard (Ed.), *Markham in Peru.* (Austin: University of Texas Press, 1991) pp.X-XI.

when in Society." On the 18th of January 1853 David Markham went to Windsor for the last time. He dined with Mr Anson on the 18th, and Mr Canning on the 19th. On the 19th and 20th he attended chapter, and got £50 voted for the parsonage at Monklands, Mr Baker's living, to which sum he and Mr Anson added £5 each. He was in London for a couple of days, and returned to Horkesley on the 22nd. From the 26th to the 28th his old friend and schoolfellow Mr Berners, with his wife and daughter, were at Horkesley; and their visit was followed by one from Mr and Mrs Drummond from January 31st to February 2nd. The last visit at Horkesley was from Willy Wickham, who arrived on the 19th of March, the day on which his uncle was taken ill, and staid until the 25th.

A memorial window to Dr Ward – the late Bishop of Sodor and Man – and David Markham's predecessor, was offered for the east end of the church by his only surviving son the Reverend W. Ward; to be executed by Wailes of Newcastle. The tracery of the window, and the drip stone were so dilapidated that considerable repairs were necessary, which were done at the sole expense of the Rector, and completed on December 11th 1852, when the stained glass window, representing the crucifixion, was put up.

In October 1852 considerable repairs were found to be necessary in the flooring of the library and study at the Rectory, and the opportunity was taken of substituting bow windows with sashes, for the French windows opening down to the ground. This proved to be a great improvement. The work was begun on October 15th, and finished on November 17th, on which day David Markham got back into his study and dressing room.

In these last months he took much interest in the work of restoration that Mr Birch[113] was conducting at Wiston church. On the 12th of January 1853 he walked down to Wiston with his daughter Gena and Captain Quin "to see what Birch was doing. He has made great improvements, and the church bids fair to be one of the most interesting in the neighbourhood." On the 14th Mr Ward came to see the new window at Horkesley, and

[113] Author's Note: Mr Birch died 27 December 1887.

David Markham walked with him to Wiston. On the 24th he was again at Wiston, on the 27th he walked down there with Mr Berners; and on the 4th of February he went there once more with Captain Quin, when he found the new apse, on the foundations of an old one discovered by Mr Birch, to be six feet high. This was David Markham's last visit to Wiston. The church has since been completed in excellent taste, and is a perfect little gem of Norman architecture.

David Markham received frequent letters from his son which gave him great pleasure. Out of one describing the Isthmus of Panama he prepared an article which was published by Dickens in *Household Words*. His son's book, which he had so admirably edited, was also published at this time. On February 16th he wrote "Mattacks (the Colchester bookseller) tells me that *Franklin's Footsteps* sells better than any other book of the kind he has ever had. He has already sold 75 copies." His last letter to his son was written in March, and the last words were "Good bye, my dear boy, come back quick and safe and well."

In November he had had an attack of gout and was unable to do any part of the service on November 28th and December 5th, but on every other Sunday from October 3rd 1852 to March 13th 1853 he preached and did part of the services, while on two Sundays in October, in the absence of Mr Edwards, he performed both services and preached twice. He had indeed been more free from gout than in several previous years.

But on the night of the 18th of March he had an attack. [He was] confined to his room, and the attack continued. He was ill for the next nine days. On Thursday the 31st of March 1853 the disease attacked the heart. His wife was with him; but he only had time to gasp "my poor wife," and "bless my dear children," and he was gone.

To him there could be no suddenness, for his life was one of daily preparation. But to those he left behind the blow was crushing – when the news spread in the parish, to Colchester, to Windsor, to Yorkshire, the first feeling was one of consternation. David Markham was loved dearly by many friends who could ill spare his kind and helpful advice; the pleasure of his society; his useful, unselfish, untiring aid and assistance in their undertakings. He was buried on April 7th 1853 in the churchyard of Great Horkesley, under the shadow of the tower, in the same grave with his mother, and the same grave stone serves for both.

CONCLUSION

With the death of David Markham Lord de Grey[114] gave the living of Great Horkesley to a nephew of Lady de Grey, the Reverend John Balfour Magenis.[115] He appears to have been an unsuitable candidate, heavily in debt and with few qualifications. The author states that "It was found that no satisfactory arrangement could be made with him respecting the school, and all the good work was neglected or wholly disused." Worse were a number of changes he made to the church itself.

> But he committed a shocking act of ignorant vandalism. He destroyed the chancel arch, which was the oldest and most interesting part of the church, to put in its place a poor pointed arch, as more in keeping with the rest of the church. He also put an ugly stove into the centre of the chancel, just in front of the communion rails, and opened a small door near the west end of the north aisle, which had hitherto been blocked by the deal pews.
>
> On his death two windows in the chancel, which had been put in by Mr Markham, were taken out to make room for two stained glass windows put up to Mr Magenis's memory, by his brothers. They are poor and in bad taste, and the removal of Mr Markham's windows was a most improper proceeding.

---

114 Henry George Grey, third Earl Grey (1802-1894). Earl Grey enjoyed an active political life devoted to reform. Early in his career he backed Catholic Emancipation, Parliamentary Reform and the abolition of British colonial slavery. As Secretary for War (1835-39) he attempted to reform the lives of the rank and file through improved conditions, regimental savings banks and libraries, although his efforts met with a mixed reception. He later served as colonial secretary and continued, through his later life, to actively question British policies towards its colonial possessions. Peter Boroughs, "Grey, Henry George, third earl Grey (1802-1894)" *Oxford Dictionary of National Biography*. (Oxford: Oxford University Press, 2004) Online Ed.

115 Author's Note: He was the son of Richard Magenis of Warrington, Co. Down, by Lady Elizabeth Cole, daughter of the 1st Earl of Enniskillen.

When the Reverend Magenis died on June 1st 1862 matters in the parish went from bad to worse. The patronage of Great Horkesley passed to Lord de Grey's daughter, Lady Cowper, and her choice was the Reverend John Steel.[116] He is described by Clements Markham as "a man advanced in years, needy, negligent, and ill tempered. His neglect came to such a pitch that for two years there was no school at all open in the parish." And as for the church he did nothing to it, "...never even cleaned it."

Due to the failure of the Reverend Steel it was necessary for measures to be taken to try and save the school from complete neglect. The school was brought under the management of Clements Markham, the Rector, Churchwardens and a committee of five to be elected by the subscribers of the school. It was decided that the Bible would form the basis of instruction and that the school would be conducted according to the principles and designs of the *National Society for Promoting the Education of the Poor in the Principles of the Church of England*. David Markham's will specified maintenance of a school, but did not specify the Infant School. Therefore, to save money, the new Rector and Churchwardens wished to build the new National School upon the same land and at the expense of the Infant School. In the end the new National School was built alongside the Infant School, with a door connecting the two. The schoolmaster's house was also erected close by, with the result that the Infant school lost much of its playground area.[117]

---

[116] Author's Note: Mr Steel was born about 1800. He was at Cambridge, but never took his Master's degree, and was ordained in 1824. From 1827 to 1862 he was Perpetual Curate of Cowbit in Lincolnshire, worth £245 a year. By his first wife he had a son – John Steel (junior) born about 1836, who was at Balliol College Oxford, M.A. 1865, Curate of Welby 1860-63, of Horkesley 1863-69; and since 1869 Vicar of Harold in Bedfordshire, a living given to him by Lady Cowper. By his second wife, who came with him to Horkesley, he had two sons who died at Marlborough School in 1870. Mr Steel died on the 16th of October 1876. He had been tutor to Lady Cowper's sons.

[117] Author's Note: The Schoolmaster's name is Page, a trained teacher, and his wife, also a well trained teacher, takes the Infant School which is kept up. Their daughter is pupil teacher. Average school attendance was: 1874–39, 1875-77, 1876-79, 1877-86, 1879-89, 1880-97, 1881-110.

With the death of the Reverend John Steel in 1876 Lady Cowper presented the Living of Great Horkesley to the Reverend John Storr.[118] The Churchwardens at this time were a Mr Green, at Brewood Hall, and Mr Dyer at Park Farm. A Miss Dyer played the harmonium in church and Charles Polley, the long time Clerk, remained in his role until his death in 1880. In 1878:

> ...a building on the Causeway was bought from the Primitive Methodists, and converted into a club room, 30ft by 18 ft. Purchase money £66, and £80 for alterations, furniture, etc. It was opened in October 1878, and lengthened in 1880. The Club has a library, periodicals, games, and tea and coffee. Manageress – Mahala Peechey. [Subscriptions – Lady Cowper £20, Capt. Kelso £30, Mr Storr £15, Mr Sadler £5, Mr Clements Markham £5,]. In 1899 the Club was self supporting. In 1882 an organ (costing £280, a sum raised by subscriptions) was placed in Great Horkesley Church; against the east wall of the N.E. Chantry.

It would appear that the parish of Stillingfleet, where David Markham began his career, faired much better, benefiting from a series of very capable individuals.[119] One of these, the Reverend W.A. Wightman,[120] acknowledged the positive influence that David Markham had had during his time at Stillingfleet:

> The people at Stillingfleet continually say such and such a thing was done in Mr Markham's time, and succeeding Vicars have been indebted to him for building the greater part of the commodious vicarage in which I am now living.

---

[118] Author's Note: John Storr was the son of the Rev. Francis Storr, Vicar of Benchley in Kent, and whose mother was a Miss Holland, sister of David Markham's former Curate at Horkesley. Reverend Storr entered Holy Orders in 1867, and became Curate of Silsoe from 1867 to 1869; whence he removed to Flitton in Bedfordshire. On February 7th 1877 he was married, in London, to Amy Theodosia, daughter of Ralph Leycester Esq. of Toft in Cheshire.

[119] See Appendix Nineteen: Clergymen at Stillingfleet.

[120] Author's Note: William Arnett Wightman was born about 1832. He was of Caius College, Cambridge, B.A. 1854, and Minor Canon of York 1858, Curate of St. Helens (York) 1854-65, Vicar of Holy Trinity, York, 1866. He married a daughter of Mr Oldfield, the wine merchant at York. Mr Wightman is the son and grandson of medical men at Cawood. His father retired to York, where he died.

In 1876 it was necessary to undertake restoration work on Stillingfleet church, and while this was progressing a new memorial window to David Markham, his wife and two children, David and Selina, was installed in the Chancel. In similar fashion, a number of the projects which David Markham had undertook at Windsor were brought to fruition, such as the restoration of the Horse Shoe Cloisters, library and other buildings.[121]

[121] This was undertaken by Sir Gilbert Scott in 1873.

APPENDICES

APPENDIX ONE

Servants at Stillingfleet

Village Schoolmasters	- Mr. Sturdy - Mr. Bell. 1877 Master of the Ragged School at Bradford.
Clerks	- Thomas Plummer, (1826-1832) married Elizabeth, daughter of J. Buckle, Carpenter. - William Bristow, (1832-1833) drowned on December 26th, 1833 aged 55. - George Lazenby, (1833-1838) and tailor. He died July 17th 1872, aged 78.
Sexton	- George Slater (1826-1838). Also labourer at the vicarage.
Methodist Parson	- Tommy Brown. (1826-1838) Also gardener.
Garden Boy	- Henry Hutton. Became a joiner. Left the parish for many years, living near Sheffield. Married with 2 sons. Returned 1874. His brother, Robert, was coachman at Becca.
Garden Woman	- Peggy Bristow. Widow of the Clerk. She died in 1856, aged 76, and was buried on June 14th.

Washerwoman	- Sally Brown (1826-1838). Wife of Tommy Brown. They returned to Wigginton, their native place, where they had property, and died there.
Footman	- Thomas Baker (1827-1835) - William Hunter (1835-1837) - James Knot (1837-1838)
Grooms	- William Smithers (1832-1834) - James Smithers (1834-1836) - John Spencer (1836-1838)
Nurse	- Jane Morley (1828-1835) A native of Ulleshelf. On August 17th 1835, when 40, she was married to John Dodsworth, a widower with children, farmer and butcher at Kelfield. They retired to a house in Stillingfleet. She died there, aged 77, on January 21st 1872, and is buried near the gate of the churchyard leading to the bridge. - Mary Fletcher (1835-1838)
Lady's Maid	- Elizabeth Clayton (Bessie) (1830-1835). In 1834 she married John Dobson, shoemaker at Kelfield. - Anne Armytage (1835-1838) A very handsome woman, married and kept a private hotel in Brook Street. Mrs. Lillyman.
Cook	- Elizabeth Kirby (1830-1834) - Jane Jagger (1834-1838) Married to John Sledge in 1838. He was born in 1810, son of Francis Sledge (born 1780, died 1831). John Sledge had landed property. John Sledge died June 16th 1848.

Housemaid	- Mary Appleyard (1830-1834)
	- Mary Birdsall (1834) A native of Ulleskelfe. She married Spencer and lived at Stillingfleet, next door to the Huttons.
	- Mary Wilson (1835)
	- Ann Moyser (1836-1838)
Kitchen Maid	- Mary Spencer (1830-1835
	- Elizabeth Cooper
	- Mary King
	- Jane Coates
Nursery Maid	- Eliza Haw (1830-1840) Grand child of Molly Haw, who lived in the Gale, and smoked a clay pipe. Eliza married the gamekeeper at Moreby, and died in York hospital.
Working in the house	- Hannah Kirby

APPENDIX TWO

Dogs at Stillingfleet and Horkesley

Bronte	1830-1835.	A Newfoundland.
Rollo	1835-1842.	A sort of poodle, the dearest and cleverest of dogs, and could do every kind of trick. Some brute at Horkesley broke his leg by throwing stones, and he died. Buried under the clump of birches in the glebe at Horkesley.
Norna		A Blood Hound.
Keeper		A brown and white spaniel.
Gip		A fat spaniel, lived in the housekeeper's room.
Charley	1850-1852.	Mrs. Markham's dog. A spaniel. Buried under the birches.

APPENDIX THREE

Descriptions of Local Families

The Dodsworths of Kelfield

Matthew Dodsworth (laborer) of Westow, had a son, Leonard Dodsworth, who settled at Kelfield, and married Christiana Dutton of Poppleton. Their children were Elizabeth born 1797, John born 1799, and Matthew, a showmaker born in 1804.

John Dodsworth became a butcher at Kelfield and also a farmer. He married and had five children. On August 17th 1835 he married, secondly, in Stillingfleet church, Jane Morley, the ceremony being performed by Dr. Milner L.L.D. The Dodsworths gave up the business after about 20 years, and retired to a house in Stillingfleet, where Jane died on January 21st 1872, aged 77. John Dodsworth then went to live with his daughter Mrs. Gamble, and died at her farm on the road to Kelfield on July 22nd, aged 76. His children were:

Mary Anne. Married to Robert Gamble, a farmer, and has three daughters. One of them, Mrs.Poole, lives in the house formerly occupied by her grandparents John and Jane Dodsworth. She died 3 February 1893 aged 73. Robert Gamble died 13th April 1891 aged 76.

Leonard. Married and has a daughter. He has current and gooseberry gardens, and is famous for his early potatoes. His wife died 11th May 1893, aged 54.

John. Succeeded his father in the same house at Kelfield, as butcher and farmer. A widower with a son John, born in 1857, and three daughters, one of them wife of Mr. Barker schoolmaster at Kelfield.

Charles. Succeeded to his uncle matthew (who died in 1873) in his trade of shoemaker at Kelfield.

Matthew. A farmer at Kelfield, married.

Dobsons of Kelfield

John Dobson, shoemaker of Kelfield, married Elizabeth Clayton, in Stillingfleet church, on February 6th 1834. She died in 1846, and he in 1868, after marrying again. She had five children:

John. Settled in Australia.

Thomas. Went to Canada but did not succeed. He returned and lived at Riccall.

Frank. Page to the Reverend D. Markham. In 1850 apprenticed to a joiner in York, by Mr. Markham. Settled in Canada and married.

William. Linendraper's man in York. Tailor, in Pavement.

Mary Anne.

Huttons of Stillingfleet

Henry Hutton (laborer) of Stillingfleet married, in 1816, Sarah Buckle. Mrs. Hutton died on August 13th 1876 aged 88. Their children were:

Robert – Steward in the 'Antelope'. Many years coachman to Colonel Markham of Becca. Married Miss Wood, a daughter of the butcher of Aberford. Then kept a public house at Melton Mowbray, the 'Bishop's Blaize.'

William – Also in service. Butler at Parlington. Died at Aberford.

John – A cripple, lived at home with his mother. He died in 1873.

Henry – Apprenticed to a carpenter at Ullesshelf. Then went to an uncle at Glossof in Lancashire. Then for some years near Sheffield, as a house carpenter. On the death of his brother

John, he returned to Stillingfleet, and built a workshop behind the old cottage. He married and had two sons, one settled at Wellington in New Zealand, the other working at a dock in London. The former came home to Stillingfleet in 1877. 1879 went back to Sheffield.

George – A tailor at Escrich. Died.

Sarah – Mrs. Bell, lives at Morely Farm. In 1881-82 her married daughter lived in an old cottage of the Huttons at Stillingfleet. In 1896 she went to live at the lodge on the road from Stillingfleet to Morely, at the turn of the road leading to Acaster ferry. Two sons in Stillingfleet.

APPENDIX FOUR

Descendants of Oldfield Bowles

- First descendant is missing due to pages lost.

Henry — Colonel in the Coldstream Guards. In 1819 he married Charlotte daughter of L. Starkie Esq. of Huntroyd. Secondly in 1858, Miss Fanny Brandling. He died Oct. 30th 1861, leaving:

> Henry - In the Guards, born 1828. In 1851 he married Fenella, daughter of Lord Fitzthardinge.
>
> Edward – In the Rifle Brigade.
>
> Frances – Married on August 22nd 1865 to the honourable and Reverend L. Denman.
>
> Charlotte – died 1877.
>
> Harriette – married in 1858, Richard son of H. Streatfield of Chidingston. Died 1877.
>
> Emma – Married in 1858 to the Honourable and Reverend Bligh son of the Earl of Darnley.

Edward — Lieutenant E.J.C.S. Died in India.

Mary — Married in 1815 to Wm. P. Johnson Esq of Wolton House in Cumberland. She died in April 1864, he in September 1865. Their children were:

> George Johnson – Born in 1816. In 1842 he married Frederica, daughter of Colonel Sir Fred Hankey.
>
> Edward – Curate of Farnborough, Archdeacon of Chester. Vicar of Northenden. 1876 Bishop of Calcutta.

Gertrude

Lucy – Died 1867.

Harriette – Married to her cousin Charles Brandling. She died on 5th October 1864.

Anne — Married to the Right Honorable Wm. Sturges Bourne, of Testwood co. Hants. She died in June 1850, leaving an only child.

Anne – Born April 1st 1809.

Emma — Married to the Reverend Ralph Brandling, of Gosforth in Northumberland. Children were:

Charles – Of Middleton Lodge, Co. York, married his cousin Henrietta Armytage. They had two children, Charles, who married the Countess of Jersey, daughter of Sir Robert Peel, on September 12th 1865; and Harriet.

Emma – Married her cousin Charles Markham.

Mary – Married Captain Charles Bell R.N. She died on May 24th 1831. He was drowned August 8th 1844.

Elizabeth – married Lieutenant General Sir Henry Browne in 1826. He tried to poison her. She died in 1860. They had two children, Ralph, a clergyman, and Henry.

Elizabeth — Married to Wm. Markham of Becca.

Lucy — Married on April 16th 1805 to William Holbech Esq. of Farnborough. She died November 7th 1835. He died May 22nd 1856. Their children were:

Hugh - Born in 1814, in 1838 married to Jane daughter of Viscount Bridport, and died in 1849.

Charles - born in 1816. Charles was at Baliol in 1838 (B.A.) and received an M.A. in 1841. Rector of Farnborough (1842) and Archdeacon of Coventry (1873-87). He succeeded his father in 1856. He married his cousin Laura Armytage and has nine children:

> Walter – Born in 1845.
>
> Edward – Born in 1846. Lieutenant R.N.
>
> William – Born in 1850. A Clergyman. Orange River, Free State, Archdeacon of Kimberely.
>
> Hugh – Born in 1859. Priest 1883. Rector of Whittington.
>
> Jessie
>
> Lucy Gertrude
>
> Agnes Mary
>
> Annie Laura
>
> Godfrey – At Eton.

Henry - Born 1818. In the 60th Rifles. He died at Dublin August 26th 1849.

Mary - Born December 3rd 1806.

Lucy - Married her cousin Wm. Markham. She was born June 1808.

Laura - Born in 1809. In 1846 she married John Hardy Esq. of Dunstall Hall, Co. Stafford and has:

> Reginald – Born 1848. Married Mary, daughter of Captain Gladstone, and has three children, Bertram (born 1877), Eustace (Born 1880) and Leonard (Born 1882).
>
> Lawrence – Born 1854. In business. Low Moor Iron Works.
>
> Henry – Born 1850. Rifle Brigade.
>
> Gerald – Born 1852. A Barrister.

Frances - Died in 1850.

Jane -A twin with her sister Emma, married on December 14th 1853 to Colonel Henry Cartwright of the Grenadier Guards, M.P. for Northamptonshire. Had five children:

Henry Aubrey – Born 1858.

Edward – Born 1860.

Lucy

Maud

William Digby – Born Fenruary 11, 1865.

Emma - Died February 1882.

Laura Gertrude

Married to Frederick Moysey Esq. who was born on February 28th 1781 (son of Judge Moysey by a daughter of Lord Poltimore). In 1847 he bought Rickhurst Mead, in Kent. Mrs. Moysey died childless on May 20th, 1854; and Mr. Moysey on June 8th 1863.

Frances

Married to Edward Golding, Esq. of Maiden Erlagh Co. Berkshire, on November 7th 1807, brother of Charles Golding who married Charlotte Palmer. They had:

Edward Golding – Rector of Brinton, in Bewrshire. He married Louisa Elliot and had ten children.

Frances Emma – Married, on August 8th 1843, to Reverend Matthew T. Farrer, Rector of Addington in Surrey. She died on September 3rd, 1844.

Mary Anne – married to St. George Lowther. He died on March 10th 1871. They had two children, Launcelot, and another whose name was not recorded by the author.

Laura – Married in 1847 to Lieutenant Colonel Cator (Lennard), and died in 1850. (He married secondly Miss Hallam). Two children:

Penelope – born in 1848, married in September 1875 to William Packe, Esq.

Laura – Mrs. Hoare. Married William Hoare (brewer), Summerhill Cranbrook.

Charles Oldfield Bowles

Of North Aston. Born August 30th 1785. He died July 4th 1862. On April 9th 1815 he married Elizabeth Montague, daughter of Lord Rokeby. They had five children:

Charles – Born 1816. He married Martina, daughter of Dr. Grant C.J.C.S. and widow of Captain Jackson. He died in the Crimea.

Charles

Arthur

Mary

Henry Oldfield – Born 1818. He married Barbara, daughter of Dr. Pelham Warren M.D. They had four children:

Laura

Lucy

Henry (Rifle Brigade)

(name not given)

Edward – Born in 1825. In the 60th Rifles. In 1858 he married Jane, daughter of Reverend H. Hutton. Their children were:

Edward (at Winchester)

Alice

Ethel

Jane Lydia – Married Baron Grump von Freudenstein. Died 1859. The had one son, Ernest.

Laura Gertrude – Married September 1863 to major James Greenwood. He died September 26th 1870.

APPENDIX FIVE

The Sadlers of Horkesley

Mr. Stebbing Sadler had five children. They were Ashton, Stebbing, Marianne, Sarah, and Isabella. Marianne married a missionary in India, Sarah married Mr. Freeland and died and Isabella died. When Mr. Sadler died in 1869, his younger son Stebbing succeeded to Old House by his father's will. He let it to Captain H. E. Beville (formerly 5th Dragoon Guards, born 1802) who died August 4th 1873, and then to his widow, who left in 1877. He had previously let it to Capt. T.G. Forbes R.N. whose wife died in 1867, aged 51.

A William Sadler of Little Horkesley is mentioned in a survey of the time of Henry VIII. The first mention of the Sadler family, in the Horkesley Register, is the entry of the burial of Christopher Sadler in 1625. His son Christopher Sadler was the parson's Churchwarden in 1635. He died in 1698, aged 53. His son William had a son William baptized in 1706. In 1719 his daughter Lettice Sadler married Ralph Polley. Another Christopher Sadler was buried in 1741; and another was born in 1746. On October 4th 1763 Mary Sadler married Reverend John Carr, Curate at Great Horkesley.

William Sadler = Hannah Edwards
b.1728 d.1813 — d. 1767

Rev. Wm. Sadler = Sarah
b.1764 d. 1837 — b.1767 d. 1851

Rev. Nash White = Anne (Vicar of Aveney; d. 1854)
Mrs Elwes
William Stubbing Sadler = Margaret (b. 1803 d. 1860; b.1801 d. 1860)

Marianne = Rev. Mr. Little (Missionary in India)
Sarah = Parker Freeland (b. 1832 d. 1856)
Stebbing = Miss Ellis (Daugh.of Redor of Langham)
Isabella (b. 1836 d. 1855)
Ashton

APPENDIX SIX

Owners of Little Horkesley

1. Robert Godebold — Married to a Reginilda. The author here makes a reference to Edward the Confessor.
2. Robert
3. Robert
4. _ _ilif ?
5. Walter de Horkesley — The author here makes a reference to Henry III.
6. Sir Robert de Horkesley
7. Sir William de Horkesley — Married Emma. Died in 1322. Little Horkesley passed to Swinborne by fine in 1324.
8. Robert de Swinborne — Took it over in 1324.
9. William de Swinborne — Founded the first church. Married Philippa
10. Sir Robert Swinborne — Married to Jane Botetort. He died October 19th 1391.
11. Nicholas Berners — The property passed to Nicholas through his wife

    Margery, daughter of Sir Robert Swinborne. Nicholas died in 1441.
12. Sir William Fynderne — Passed to Sir William through marriage to Catherine, daughter of Sir William Berners. He died in 1462.
13. Sir William Fynderne — Died 1515.
14. William Fynderne

15. Thomas Fynderne	Died 1523. He married Bridget, daughter of Sir. William Waldegrave. She died September 1549.
16. Anne Tyrell	Succeeded to Horkesley and married Sir Roger Wentworth. She died 1524.
17. Sir John Wentworth	Died in 1567.
18. Henry Wentworth	
19. John Wentworth	Of Little Horkesley. Died 1588
20. John Wentworth	Died 1613.
21. Sir John Wentworth	Sold Little Horkesley to Sir Humphrey Winch
22. Sir John Denham	
23. John Denham	A poet.
24. George Withers	Purchased Little Horkesley in 1651.
25. John Fielder	1653.
26. Azariah Husbands	Purchased Little Horkesley in 1660. He was married to Elizabeth, daughter of J. Fielder of Barrow Court, widow of R. Knight of Chawton. He died in 1666.
27. Edward Husbands	Built a large brick house at Little Horkesley. He married Ann daughter of J. Burroughs of Ipswich, who died 1733 at age 77. Edward died January 20th 1736 aged 79.
28. Reverend James Husbands	Vicar of Little Horkesley and Fordham. Died 1749 aged 57.
29. Anne	Married R. Glanville.
30. Anne	Married to Dr. Wm. Blair M.D. of Lavenham

31. Mrs. Warren	
32. Rev. John C. Blair Warren	Incumbent 1826-1856. married to Harriet Eliza, daughter of General Watson of Westwood. John died January 8th, 1856.
33. Mr. Bourdillon	Succeeded to Little Horkesley. The author lists it as being 963 acres and worth £1990.

APPENDIX SEVEN

Lords of the Manor of Great Horkesley

1.	Geoffrey le Scrope	Died 1340.
2.	Henry Le Scrope	Died 1391.
3.	Stephen le Scrope	
4.	Sir John Scrope of Masham	Died 1455.
5.	Thomas Scrope	Died 1475.
6.	Thomas Scrope	Died 1494. Married Elizabeth, daughter of the Marquis Montacute. Elizabeth died in 1515.
7.	Alice Scrope	Heiress.
8.	William Shelley	A relation of the Scropes, he received the estate from the crown in 1540. He died in 1550.
9.	William Shelley	Died in 1597.
10.	John Carrill	Came into possession of the estate in 1604.
11.	Sir Paul Bayning.	Baron Bayning bought the estate from the Shelleys. He died in 1629.
12.	Paul Viscount Bayning	Died in 1638.
13.	Anne	Married Aubrey, 20th Earl of Oxford.
14.	Nicolas Freeman	A clothier at Dedham, he had the estate from 1712.
15.	Nicolas Freeman	
16.	Robert Freeman	
17.	John Freeman	
18.	John Freeman	
19.	Mr. Cuddon	1838.

APPENDIX EIGHT

Rectors of Great Horkesley

1.1336. Richard Oliver
1349 - Walter de Salcote
1372 - William de Welton
1382 - John Stacey
1385 - Stephen Ingram
1392 - John Brokket/John Stacey

1413 - Robert Symeon
1426 - William Golding/Robert Thorpe
1481 - Thomas Moyse
1484 - Richards Hygs
1488 - James Daven/John Rolo

1503 - Ralph Daniell
1549 - Richard Tomlynson (Patron Bishop Bonnor)/ Thomas Hulson
1559 - Robert Coates (Patron J. Lucas)
1562 - Thomas Scotte (Patron J. Lucas)
1580 - John Brownde (Patron J. Lucas)

1617 - William Eyre
1642 - Thomas Eyre
1683 - Robert Harrison (Patron Earl of Kent)

1732 - John Morse (Tombstone in Chancel floor)
1747 - George Henry Rooke D.D.
1754 - James Yorke (Bishop of Ely)
1756 - John Browne D.D.

1771 - John Cock D.D. Marble tablet over chancel door. Died in 1796 aged 80.

1796 - Philip Yorke (Prebendary of Ely) Son of the Bishop. Aged 46.

1817 - William Ward D.D. Bishop of Sodor and Man aged 77.

1838 - David F. Markham Canon of Windsor. Aged 53.

1853 - J.B. Magenis (Patron Earl de Grey)

1862 - John Steel

1876 - John Storr

APPENDIX NINE

Monuments in Great Horkesley Church

On the Floor

1. Chancel: Before the vestry door. A slate slab, arms and crest of Gibbs of Horkesley Park. Inscription in memory of Samuel who died on October 8th 1692, aged 67; of his son Samuel who died March 3rd 1724 aged 69; and of his grandson Samuel who died February 29th 1739 aged 28.
2. Chancel: Opposite, on south side. A slate slab to the memory of Dr. Morse, Rector of Great Horkesley 1732 to 1747, and Prebendary of Lichfield.
3. Chancel: West of the Gibbs Monument and a step lower; stone slab to the memory of Dr. Cock, Rector of Great Horkesley 1771 to 1796, and of Debden. He died 30th January 1796, aged 80.
4. Chancel: Centre of the aisle, slab with brass all picked out. A cross and inscription round, to Richard Oliver, Rector 1326.
5. Nave: Centre of the aisle. Slate slab. In memory of Christopher Sadler, gent, of Great Horkesley who died October 17th 1698 aged 53 years, of his wife Hannah who died 5th February 1719 aged 59, and of William Sadler who died 15th January 1753, aged 69.
6. Nave: A slab west of the Sadlers, with a place where has been a brass plate.

On the Walls

1. Over the Chancel door: A white marble scroll hanging from a shelf with an urn above. "In memory of John Cock D.D. many

years Rector of this Parish, and also of Debden in this county, who died 30th January 1796, aged 80 years.

2. Between the windows on south side of the nave: A white marble tablet – "The Reverend Philip Yorke A.M. the fourth son of the late Bishop of Ely, Prebendary of Ely Cathedral, and for twenty one years Rector of this parish, departed this life on the 29th day of May 1797 (a note added questions 1817?), aged 47 years. This tablet was erected at the expense of his parishioners, as a public memorial of their loss, as a tribute of affectionate respect to their beloved pastor, and as an expression of gratitude and resignation to the will of Divine Providence, in having so long vouchsafed unto them a faithful and exemplary minister, who watched for their souls, whose faith follow, considering the end of his conversation Jesus Christ, the same yesterday, today, and for ever."

Twere vain his Christian virtues to reveal
Their praise shall live in this our hearts' record
O may the love and deep regrets we feel
Witness our union with him in the Lord

3. Between the windows on the north side of the nave: A white marble tablet: "Sacred to the memory of Elizabeth, wife of Thomas George Forbes, Captain R.N. who died 18th March 1867, aged 50 years" In thee O Lord have I put my trust.

4. On the north chancel wall, east of the vestry door: A black marble slab and on it a brass tablet to the memory of Mrs Elizabeth Mure, Mother of the Reverend David F. Markham Rector of Great Horkesley.

5. In the N.E. Chapel, under the memorial windows to the memory of the Reverend David F. Markham, put up by the neighbouring clergy and those of Windsor; a brass plate "To the blessed memory of the Reverend David F. Markham, Rector of the Parish, who deceased March 31st 1853, aged 53.

Windows

1. East window to the memory of Dr. W. Ward, Bishop of Sodar and Man. Rector 1817 to 1838; a Crucifixion, with arms of the See impaling his own, in the tracery. Put up by his son the Reverend W. Ward 1852 (Dec).
2. Two windows to the memory of the Reverend D. F. Markham in the N.E. Chapel.
3. Two windows to the memory of the Reverend J.B. Magenis on either side of the chancel door, south wall, put up by his three surviving brothers.
4. A window at the west end of the north aisle to the memory of the two sons of Reverend J. Steel, Rector from 1862 to 1876. They died at Marlborough school.

APPENDIX TEN

List of Prints of Westminster Men Given to the Elizabethan Club by Clements R. Markham

Elizabeth

1552-1609	Martin Heton, Bishop of Ely
1555-1604	Reverend Cedes, Dean of Worcester
1559-1621	John King, Bishop of London
1.1652.	Peter Smart, the Puritan
1573-1631	Sir Dudley Carleton
1574-1637	Ben Johnson
1577-1617	Tom Coryat, the Traveller
1582-1635	Reverend Corbet, Bishop of Norwich
1588-1672	Brian Duffa, Bishop of Winchester
1591-1670	John Hacket, Bishop of Lichfield
1591-1679	Henry King, Bishop of Chichester
1593-1632	George Herbert, Poet
1597-1684	George Morley, Bishop of Winchester
1602-1685	Sir John Marsham, Chronologist

James I

1613-1666	Sir John Glynne, Chief Justice
1.1634.	Thomas Randolph, Poet
1606-1695	Richard Busby, Head Master
1608-1684	Ed. Rainbow, Bishop of Carlisle
1611-1642	William Cartwright, Poet
1621-1682	Heneage Finch, 1st Earl of Nottingham
1622-1677	Martin Clifford, Wit and Poet
1.1686.	J. Dolben, Archbishop of York

Charles I

1630-1703	Sir J. Millington, M.D.
1631-1700	John Dryden, Poet
1632-1704	John Locke, Philosopher
1633-1716	Robert South, Preacher
1636-1702	Thomas Gale, Dean of York
1638-1711	Benjamin Woodroffe, Canon of Christ Church
1638-1711	Thomas Knife, Head Master
1640-1727	George Hooper, Bishop of Bath and Wells
1647-1710	Henry Aldrich, Dean of Christ Church
1648-1724	Humphrey Prideaux, Dean of Norwich
1649-1713	Charles Hickman, Bishop of Derry
1649 -	Nathaniel Lee, Dramatic Poet

Charles II

1658-1742	Lancelot Blackburn, Archbishop of York
1660-1728	White Kennet, Bishop of Peterborough
1661-1715	C. Montagu, Earl of Halifax
1661-1732	F. Atherbury, Bishop of Rochester
1663-1712	William King, L.L.D Civilian
1.1719.	George Smalridge, Bishop of Bristol
1663-1707	G. Stepney, Diplomatist
1665-1725	F. Gastnell, Bishop of Chester

Charles II, Con't

1665-1721	Matthew Prior, Poet
1667-1735	G. Granville, Lord Landsdowne
1668-1747	Michael Maittaire, Greek Scholar
1673-1718	Nicholas Ronu, Poet
1675-1728	John Friend, M.D., Physician
1675-1743	William Shippen, Parliamentary Orator
1684-1725	C. Lord Whitworth
1682-1760	Willis Brown, Archaeologist

James II

1686-1746	Sir J.Hanmer, Speaker
1686-1750	Aaron Hill, Poet

William III

1688-1764	R. Boyle, Earl of Shannon
1690-1763	John, Earl Granville
1690-1741	Baron Wainwright, Irish Judge
1697-1730	Robert Booth, M.P. for Bodmin
1699-1745	C. Este, Bishop of Waterford
1700-1758	John Dyer, Poet
1703-1782	Thomas Newton, Bishop of Bristol

Anne

1704-1793	William Murray, Earl of Mansfield
1706-1760	Isaac H. Browne, Poet
1707-1762	J. Boyle, Earl of Cork
1708-1788	Charles Wesley
1709-1792	Sir Cardley Wilmot, Chief Justice
1.1794.	R. Robinson, Archbishop of Armagh
1711-1776	R. Drummond, Archbishop of York
1713-1771	G. Sharpe, Greek and Hebrew Scholar

George I

1714-1766	William Friend, Dean of Canterbury
1721-1803	G. Leveson Gower, Marquis of Stafford
1721-1788	Th. Sheridan, Father of Reverend Brinsley
1.1791.	Joseph Wilcocks, Man of Letters
1726-1814	Sir William Dolben, M.P.
1727-1796	D. Murray, Viscount Stormont
1.1806.	J. Barnard, Bishop of Limerick

George II

1728-1813	Spencer Madan, Bishop of Peterborough
1729-1807	William Markham, Archbishop of York
1730-1799	William M. Cackerode, Man of Letters
1731-1819	William C. Jennings, Virtuoso
1731-1800	William Cowper, Poet
1732-1794	John Hinchliffe, Bishop of Peterborough
1732-1818	Warren Hastings, Governor General of India
1732-1794	George Coleman, Poet
1732-1811	Neville Maskelyne, Astronomer
1733-1788	William Digby, Dean of Durham

George II Con't

1734-1806	3rd Duke of Richmond
1735-1789	George Byng, M.P. for Middlesex
1736-1812	John Home Tooke
1737-1794	Edward Gibbon, Historian
1737-1809	Charles Agar, Archbishop of Dublin
1738-1809	William Duke of Portland, Prime Minister
1739-1826	Sir J. Aubrey, Lord of Treasury
1740-1778	A.M. Toplady, Calvinist Divine
1741-1795	Reverend G. Butt
1743-1827	Samuel Goodenough, Bishop of Carlisle
1745-1819	Cyril Jackson, Dean of Christ Church
1749-1813	John Randolph, Bishop of London
1749-1825	Gerard Andreves, Dean of Canterbury
1751-1818	William Jackson, Bishop of Oxford
1753-1829	Robert Naves, Archdeacon of Stafford

George III

1764-1847	George Byng, M.P. for Middlesex
1757-1829	C. Abbot, Lord Colchester (Speaker)
1764-1819	Ch. Duke of Richmond
1768-1854	1st Marquis of Anglesey
1756-1832	Sir Everard Home
1769-1846	William Carey, Bishop of St. Asaph
1770-1854	Sir Francis Burdett
1773-1818	Matthew J. Lewis, Monk
1780-1866	Marquis of Landsdowne
1791-1860	Ch. Duke of Richmond
1792-	Earl Russell, Prime Minister
	R. Southey, Poet

APPENDIX ELEVEN

Descriptions of Churches in Devonshire and Oxfordshire in the Property of the Dean and Chapter of Windsor, Made During an Inspection 1847

Plymton St. Mary's

A good perpendicular church of 5 aisles. The 2 outer aisles extending half the length. Good monument of the 15th century in the 5th aisle, Sedilla and piscina. Fine east window Parker monuments in the chancel. Fine monument in N. aisle like that in S. aisle with recumbent figure, but earlier.

Many rich people in the parish, the poor in good condition and well looked after. Church 96 feet wide, 133 long. The church in excellent repair. Two good porches Northern and Southern, the situation beautiful. Room for 8 or 900 [?] in the porch. 3 full services in the parish, service at Sparkwell 5 miles off. Curate paid by curate aid. Subscription School 75 children. Population 3000, 7 villages. Clothing club for 500 people. £300 worth of clothing. Ridway school established of 170 children. £60 a year subscribed, with an endowment of £500.

Plymton St. Maurice

An interesting church, older than P. St. Mary but in poor condition. The east window destroyed and restored in wood. Pulpit and desk very beautiful. Old stone pulpit and pedestal. Windows perpendicular. Piscina in south aisle. Accommodation for 400. Perpetual curacy. Incumbent Dr. Williams age 46, presented in 1845. Stoup at north door. Extent of parish 203 acres. Population 700-940. poor rates upon ½ the rent is 2/6 in the pound. High way rate [?] on the whole rental. Endowment: 1 field purchased by Queen Anne's County called Queen Anne's meadow, 1.22.6 £

orchard 1:16 title free acres 1.1.30 in the parish. Dr Williams' house very pleasantly situated, capable of being bought as a parsonage house: it would be an admirable arrangement.

Brixton Chapel

Perpendicular church in decent repair, pewed after the the most approved G III fashion. One good window in the south aisle blocked up by a monument. Floor dry and decently paved. Roof pierced for dormer windows. Room for 300. Stoup in porch.

Ancient house to the north having the appearance of the vicarage house. On talking to Mr Low of Coffleet, whom we found at his ____ _____ boat house on the Yealm, a gentlemanly and sensible old man, it appears that the priest's house was actually sold with the tithes to release the land tax in 1802, to Mr Spratt, who cannot take it down till the incumbent dies!!!

Plymstock

A perpendicular church with high _____; _____ a fine organ screen, much patched, is erected between the chancel and nave, probably originally belonging to the priory. A circular Norman font with curious canopy, raised much above the original position and modernized. Ugly sky lights. Church and chancel in good repair, capable of containing 500 people. Many wealthy people in the parish.

Sampford Spinney

Curious church of late period, with very beautiful tower and crockated pinnacles. Condition bad, ill paved, damp, and badly arranged. Mr Pearse, the incumbent, lives at Ivy Bridge, a distance of 17 miles. Curate lives at Tavistock, 4 miles distant. Service one full one on alternate Sundays. Holy communion monthly. Vicarage house distant 2/3 of a mile, chapel ½ a mile. Chapel not well attended, about 30 or 40, population 300. A piece of waste ground, 11 acres, adjoining the church yard with a poor house on it (probably the priest's house) in the possession of the Palvy family. Vicarage house rated at £4. Less than ½ an acre of garden. Commutation of tithe 3/5 an acre.

Shaugh

Perpendicular Church in only moderate repair. Windows wood framed. Singularly flat elliptical arches supported by slender columns. Pewing high but sound. So much white work on the walls and woodwork as to conceal numberless serious defects.

2 full services in summer, 1 in winter, communion 4 times a year. Smith and Warner's charity.

St. Germans

A fine old Norman church much mutilated but very interesting. The Eliot family has been its great marrer [sic]. Parsonage house very good and well situated, near the church. Two chapelries in the parish, Hepenford and Tideford. The former has a good house and garden, the chapel most wretched. At Tideford a very pretty perpendicular chapel, pews are, well arranged, built 1845. No house, 3 acres of Glebe, the gift of the St. German family. Miss Erskine gave £3000 to Hepenford, the Ladies Cornwallis £200. The same ladies gave £1500 to Tideford. The population 3000 equally divided among the three churches. 2 full services in each on Sundays, and monthly communion. Each chapel 4 miles from the mother church and 4 from each other. The whole parish 10,000 acres.

St. Stephen's by Saltash

A perpendicular church with wagon roof, 3 aisles, 2 of the east windows of which filled with glazed wood work. Pews high, square, and sound. A large heavy gallery projects into the church at west end, behind which is a wretched damp school room stolen from the nave. Church damp throughout, though the earth around has been, in a great measure, removed. Church capable of containing 500 persons. 2 full services, communion monthly. A fine Norman font similar to that at St. Germans. Excellent parsonage house, and pretty garden and glebe.

Deddington – In Oxfordshire

Town and church handsomely situated on a hill. Population 3700. Two hamlet attached, distant each a mile from the mother church, one east the other west of it, Hampton and Clifton. Value of the living under £200.

Church a very handsome structure of the early English style, with many later insertions, particularly in the nave. 3 Sedilias very good, and a handsome and uncommon piscine, all early English. A noble tower with highly enriched pinnacles. The parsonage house near the church. It seems a decent and well built house. The proposed site of the new school close to it. It is essential that this should be built. Dr Wilson, the present curate, has purchased the land and offers it for the purpose. No steps beyond applying to the Chapter of Windsor have yet been made towards a subscription. Christ Church has property in the parish. Windsor has Great House Farm, Hazel Hedge Farm, Tonwell Farm, and Lenden Farm.

Dr Wilson's proposed that the new church he has built at Hampton should be endowed by us and be in his patronage, is considered absurd by the inhabitants. It would be useless to unite it with Nether Worton as the distance is greater from that church than from Deddington. Mr Beding is about to build a church at Clifton, and he might as will propose propose to join it with North Aston. If these two churches are to be of any use it would be better to increase the value of Deddington, and let the presentation of them be in the Vicar. Dr Wilson confessed that he had more at heart the establishment of schools at Deddington than the endowment of Hampton. Neither Mr Field nor Mr Nibby were at home, but I received much attention from Mr Chamberlain, nephew of our late Lessee.

APPENDIX TWELVE

The Horkesley Visitation Cycle

A: 4. Tile House. The wooden houses. Dixey's. Joiner's yard.

8. Hull Lane. Mount Hall. Mrs Crabb's. Mr Daniell's. Hay Farm.

11. Lower Horkesley Green. Good's Farm. The cottages in the lane. W. Pages.

13. Post Office. The Rookery and all the cottages up the Brewood Hall lane.

16. Oratory, and all the cottages up to Vine Cottage on the same side.

B: 2. Brick Kiln Lane.

9. White House Pond. The Crown Inn. The Poor houses & cottages near pond.

10. Boxted Road. Mr Fisher Hobbs. Mr Whittaker's, and cottage between them.

14. Brewood Hall, and cottages in that lane.

17. Horkesley Hill. The Parks. Bridge Farm. Loch House.

C: 3. Union Yard. The houses in the yard. Beckwith's & Manor Farms.

5. Wood House Lane. Woodhouse and cottages in the lane.

7. Westwood Lane. Bruce and Chamberlain's cottages.

12. Horkesley Mill. Lees House, and the houses between them.

15. Vine cottage. The houses from thence to Brewood Hall Lane.

D: 1. America Hill. Seabourne's cottages. Muddy Lane.

19. Cockerill's. Nevard's. Knopp's and cottages between.

6. Pitchberry Wood. The two cottages of Mr Rooke: two of Mr Sadler's.

20. Upper Horkesley Green. John Appleby's: Woodgate's: cottages between.

18. Sprath's Marsh. The houses in the marsh and wood. The new farm.

APPENDIX THIRTEEN

Parishioners of Great Horkesley Circa 1845.

Name	Notes
Thomas Abelwhite	Labourer. Brick Kiln Lane
Widow Adkinson	Causeway.
Titus Adkinson	Bailey's. Jobber.
Widow Appleby	
Thomas Appleby	Small Farmer
William Appleby	Labourer
Isaac Appleby	Labourer
Atkins	Labourer. Bridge Lane
Alston	Brick Maker. Brick Kiln Lane
Widow Austin	Shop Keeper. Workhouse.
Bailey	Labourer. Marsh.
Balls	
William Beckwith	Farmer
Daniel Bibby	Proprietor.
Robert Bibby	Labourer.Union Yard.
Daniel Bibby	Labourer.Causeway.
Bibby	
Widow Bibby	Brewood Hall Lane
Frederick Bradbrook	Shoemaker. Causeway.
Brown	Labourer. Causeway.
Samuel Bruce	Beer shop. Yew Trees.
Biggs	Labourer. Hill Lane.
Boggis	Marsh. Shoemaker.
Widow Boggis	Marsh.
Mrs Bowers	

Name	Notes
Widow Bowers	Crown Inn.
Carver	Farmer
Clarke	Labourer
Peter Coveney	Farmer. Boxted Rd.
Jeremiah Coveney	Carpenter. Brick Kiln Lane.
James Cooke	Laborer. Causeway.
Widow Crabb	
Hilary Cream	Shoemaker. Brick Kiln Lane.
John Chamberlain	Gardener.
Thomas Chinnery	Laborer. Work House.
Samuel Cutler	Laborer. Boxted Rd.
Shepherd Daniell	Farmer. Hull Lane
Deekes	Servant. Crown Inn.
Widow Drues	Chapel.
James Drues	Laborer. Chapel.
Thomas Drues	Laborer.
Ditchfield	Policeman.
James Dixon	Mr Venningale's Laborer.
Thomas Dixon	Laborer. Boxted Rd.
John Dixon	Laborer.
William Dixon	Carpenter. Boxted Rd.
Dixon	
Dixon	Laborer. Nayland Rd.
James Dixon	Laborer. America Hill.
William Dixey	
Dixey	
Widow Finch	
Finian[?]	Laborer. Wood
Garwood	Laborer.
Widow Green	Milliner. Causeway
Thomas Green	Laborer.

Name	Notes
Robert Green	Farmer. Rookery
John Green	Proprietor. America Hill.
Thomas Green	Small farmer.
Haynes	Laborer. Wood House Lane
Widow Harland	
Thomas Harland	Laborer. Brick Kiln Lane.
Heifer	
Widow Howlett	
George Jackson	Miller
Johnson	Laborer. Hull Lane.
Captain Kelso	Horkesley Park. Wife x 2 children. Communicants, several Servants attend church & most of them communicants. Subscribes to charities.
Samuel Knopp	Farmer.Boxted Rd.
Larkrie [?]	Laborer.
Lee	Shipwright.
James Lott	Laborer. America Hill
Marshall	Single woman.
Mann	Farmer. Manor House.
Widow Mill	
John Minter	Laborer. Rector Lodge. Wife x 2 children. Communicants. Very respectable. House rent free. 1850 went as Bailiff to Mr Donne at Dedham.
Edward Minter	Laborer. Mr Kenningale's.
Edward Minter	Laborer. Mr. Knopp's
Minter	Laborer.Marsh.
Widow Minter	Shop Keeper.
Minter	Laborer. Causeway.
Minter	Laborer

Name	Notes
Frank Munson	Laborer. Causeway.
Widow Munson	
Daniel Munson	Shop keeper. Causeway.
William Munson	Laborer.Causeway.
Joe Munson	Laborer.
Benjamin Munson	Laborer. Brick Kiln Lane.
Nevard	Farmer.
Nevard	Gardener.
Nanny Nevard	Single woman.
Nice	Farmer
Pakley	Wheelwright. Causeway.
Charles Page	Jobber. Causeway.
Page	Jobber. D. Bibby's
Mr Partridge	Farmer. Brewood Hall.
Samuel Peachy	Carpenter. Causeway.
John Peachy	Laborer. Tile House.
John Polley	Laborer. White Horse.
John Polley	Laborer.
James Polley	Laborer. Chapel.
Charles Polley	laborer. Brewood Lane.
Polley	America hill.
James Potter	Laborer. Wood House Lane.
Nathaniel Potter	Laborer.
Daniel Potter	Laborer. Boxted Rd.
Pridham	Pitchberry Wood.
Widow Ratcliffe	Wood House Lane.
Ratcliffe	Laborer. Brick Kiln Lane.
Ratcliffe	Farmer. They [?] Farm
Ratcliffe	
Henry Rivers	Labourer. Causeway.
Rout	Laborer. Post Office.

Name	Notes
Mr Stebbing Sadler	Proprietor. Old House.
Widow Scholfield	Mr Kenningale's.
Henry Scholfield	Laborer. Union Yard.
Richard Scholfield	
Thomas Scholfield	
Seaborne	Laborer.
John Simpson	Carpenter. Causeway.
Thomas Simpson	Butcher.
Thomas Simpson	Butcher. Brewood Lane.
James Simpson	Carpenter
John Smith	Thatcher. Brick Kiln Lane.
John Smith (jun)	Baker. Union Yard.
Smith.	Laborer. America Hill.
Southernwood	Laborer. Mr. G. Sadler's.
Southernwood	Laborer.
William Sparkes	Laborer.
Thomas Sparkes	
Sparkes	Beershop. Boxted Rd.
Jeremiah Stannard	Farmer.Mount Hall.
William Stedman	Farmer. White Park.
James Stow	Laborer. Causeway.
Thomas Stow	Laborer. Barrack.
Widow Stow	Barrack.
Joseph Stow	
Alfred Stow	
Swann	Gardener. Pitchberry Wood.
Totman	Laborer. Bridge House.
Henry Vince	Laborer.
Henry J. Vince	Laborer.
Webber	Laborer. Causeway.
George Webber	Laborer. Brick Kiln Lane

Name	Notes
Henry Webber	Laborer. Brewood Lane.
Webber	
Samuel Welham	Laborer.
Warner	Laborer. Union Yard.
George Wenlock	Blacksmith. White House.
James Warren	Laborer. Brewood Lane.
John Warren	Laborer.
William Wilby	Laborer. Causeway.
William Wilby (jun)	Laborer.
Robert Wilby	
Thomas Wilby	
James Wisbey	Laborer. Barrack.
James Wisbey (jun)	
John Woodward	Parish Clerk.
William Woodward	
Robert Woodward	Laborer. Work House.
George Woodward	Laborer.

APPENDIX FOURTEEN

Visitors to Horkesley and Windsor

1845

Windsor:	Feb 15	Reverend J. Egerton
	Feb 16 to21	Miss Goldings
	March 7 to 17	Sir John and Lady Carden
	March 8 to 12	Lady Elizabeth Clements
	March 24 to 26	Mrs Stanfield

1846

Horkesley:	July 1 to 6	Mr and Mrs Stanfield
	July 27 to Aug 4	Sir John and Lady Carden
	Aug 4 to 14	Sir W. Milner, Gena, Laura

1848

Horkesley:	May 25 to 29	Mr Wickham
	June 15 to 20	Lady Milner and Louisa
Windsor:	July 30	Wm. M. Milner Esq.
	Aug 14	Mrs George Milner
Horkesley:	Aug 20 to 30	Reverend C. Holland
	Aug 31	Wm. Wickham
	Sept. 6 to 13	Mrs Baillie, May, Fannie
	Oct 16 to 27	Lady Elizabeth Clements
	Oct 28 to Nov 28	Mrs Goodenough & Louisa
	Dec 9 to 14	Reverend Seymour Neville
	Nov 25 to Dec 22	Miss Stapylton

1849

Horkesley:	Jan 19 to 22	Wm. Wickham
	Jan 20 to 22	Colonel Markham and Willy
	Feb 10	Wm. Wickham
	Feb 27 to March 2	Lady Carden and Laura Milner
	March 3 to 12	Wm. Wickham
	March 5 to 12	Mrs Stansfield
	March 10 to 12	Wm. M. Milner Esq.
	March 9 to 12	Mr Stansfield
	April 3	Wm Wickham
	April 5	Edwin Markham
	May 12 to June 20	Miss Laura Milner

1849 Con't

Windsor:	July 7	Wm. M. Milner Esq.
	July 11 to 19	Mrs Milner
	July 11 to Aug 10	Miss Laura Milner
	July 26 to Aug 2	Mrs J. Egerton
	Aug 2 to 10	Sir Wm Milner and Gena
	Aug 18 to 20	Lady Elizabeth Clements
Horkesley:	Nov 19 to 23	C. Carden Esq.
	Nov 22 to Dec 20	Miss Stapylton
	Dec 1 to 12	Wm. Wickham, Mr Venables
	Dec 31 to Jan 7	Miss Hollands

1850

Horkesley:	Feb 2 to 5	Wm. M. Milner Esq.
		Gena Milner
		Charles Strickland
	Feb 11	Wm. Wickham
	Feb 22 to 26	Mr and Mrs Wickham
	March 9	Wm.Wickham

Windsor:	June 29 to July 1	Lady Milner and Edith
	July 4	Sir William Milner and Laura
	July 8 to 11	Barnane Carden
	July 11	Mrs Milner
	Aug 1	Wm. Wickham
	Aug 5	Mrs Milner
	Aug 24 to 28	Mrs Baillie, May and Fanny
Horkesley:	Sept 25 to Oct 3	Lady and Miss Duncan
	Nov 9	Laura Markham
	Nov 9 to 14	Miss Stapylton
	Nov 25 to 30	Mr and Mrs Wickham
	Dec 6 to 9	Lady Elizabeth Clements
	Dec 18	Wm. Wickham

1851

Horkesley:	Jan 7 to 14	Wm and H. Wickham
	March 29 to 31	Wm M. Milner Esq
	April 4 to 16	Wm. Wickham
	April 5	George Baillie Esq.
	April 29 to May 10	Mrs Walker, Selina and Nannette
Windsor:	July 5	Mr and Mrs Milner
	July 5 to 14	Wm. Wickham
	July 8 to 14	John Markham
	July 8 to 14	Sir Wm. Milner, Louisa and Laura
	July 14 to 17	Lady Milner
		Barnane Carden
	July 19 to 21	Mrs Milner and Edith
	July 25 to 28	Mrs J. Egerton
	Aug 15 to 18	Lady Elizabeth Clements

Horkesley:	Oct 15 to 18	Henry Goodenough
	Oct 17 to 24	Wm. Wickham
	Oct 18 to 24	Lieutenant R.V. Hamilton R.N.
	Oct 20 to 24	Mr and Mrs Wickham and Leonora
	Nov 1 to 5	Captain R.R. Quin R.N.
	Dec 26	Wm. Wickham
	Dec 27	Captain R.R. Quin R.N.

1852

Horkesley	Feb 5 to 12	John Markham
	Feb 17 to 19	Capt R.R. Quin R.N.
	Feb 18 to 19	Lieutenant R.V. Hamilton R.N.
	Feb 21 to 23	Wm. Markham
	March 2 to 7	Lieut. R.V. Hamilton R.N.
	March 2 to 8	James Mure
	March 13 to 31	Capt. R.R. Quin R.N.
	March 20 to 22	Wm. M. Milner Esq.
	March 31	Wm Wickham
	April 12 to 16	Mr and Mrs Wickham
	April 15	Lord George Quin
	May 7 to 14	Mrs Mure and Emma
	May 8 to 14	Colonel Mure
	May 28	Mrs Wickham and Leonora
		Miss Lyttleton
	May 31	Lord George Quin
		(Selina's Wedding) Archdeacon Bentinck
		Frank Foljambe
		Henry Milner
		Mr and Mrs Watson
		Mr and Mrs Wickham

		Wm Wickham
		Wm Markham
		Edith Milner
	June 18 to 21	Countess of Mansfield
		Lady Elizabeth Murray
		Lady G. Murray
Windsor:	Aug 10 to 12	Major M. Wemyss R.N.A

APPENDIX FIFTEEN

Servants and Others at Horkesley

School Masters and Mistresses

1.44.	George Howlett and his wife
1.45.	Burrell and his wife.
1845-47	Salmon and his wife.
1.50.	Isaac Dracup and Sarah Newman
1.53.	Mrs Newman and Jane Barker. Mrs Newman died at Horkesley Dec. 20th 1854 aged 31.

Infant School Mistress

1.53.	Fanny Cordingley

Parish Clerk

1.50.	John Woodward.
1.53.	Charles Polley. Died 1880 aged 65.

Bailiff

1.50.	John Minter
1.53.	James Newman. He was also the gardener from 1848. Married Sarah Elliot the schoolmistress, formerly scullery maid.

Footman

1.39.	John Loveless.
1.53.	James Patey. Married Mary Atkinson. Died April 1876.

Page

1.43.	William Morley. Died 1845. Went to sea, H.M.S. Excellent. He was from Yorkshire.
1.50.	Frank Dobson. (Son of Bessy).
1.53.	William Humphreys.

Grooms

1838-39	James Patey. (Became Footman).
1.40.	Richard Channing.
1840-41	Edward Edmunds.
1841-45	Henry Curtis.
1845	James Chuch (Went to Becca).
1845-50	George Webb
1850-53	Edward Rusher

Garden Boy

1853	Charles Monson
	Wilby

Housekeeper

1838-39	Anne Armitage (and Lady's maid).
1.47.	Susannah Manley (and Lady's maid).
1847-53	Mary Atkinson (and Cook).

Lady's Maid

1847-48	Catherine Watts (Married a clerk in the P.O. at Edinburgh)
1848-53	Esther Jones (1853 went to Lady Milton).

Cook

1.53.	Mary Atkinson. She married James Patey in 1854, and retired to live with her uncle at Drax, near Selby in 1855, where she died on November 2nd 1857. She was buried Nov. 5th. Her niece (a sister's daughter) Harriet Tomlinson, had lived in the same house since her aunt's death – wife of a farm labourer. Industrious honest people, and have brought up 10 children. Eldest son a carpenter.

Nurse

1838-45	Mary Palmer

Nursery Maids

1.40.	Eliza Haw
1840-43	Matilda Crick
1843-44	Eliza Abbey
1844-	Emma Firmin
1844-45	Susan Cole
1845-47	Mary Ann Whining
1847-49	Jemima Wenlock. Daughter of George Wenlock, the blacksmith, by his wife Jemima Coveney, whom he married in 1831. Jemima Wenlock was born in 1832, and baptized on July 26th. Her father died in 1852, and her mother in 1854. Wenlock's sister, Mrs Bowtell, was Landlady of the "Rose and Crown." She married secondly a man named Bowtell. When Jemima left Mrs Quin she married a carpenter in London, and died leaving children in 1870. (66 Carlisle Street, Lambeth)
1849-52	Esther Cutler. Daughter of a labourer named Robert Cutler by his wife Anne Ward, whom he married in 1821. Esther was born in 1834, and baptized in Great Horkesley Church on October 19th.

Young Lady's Maids

1845-47	Catherine Watts. Married to a Clerk in the Post Office at Edinburgh.
1.49.	Sarah Trant.
1.52.	Jemima Wenlock. (as above).
1852-53	Esther Cutler.

Housemaids

1.42.	Maria Stratton.
1.45.	Emma Eldridge.
1845.	Mary Pearson.
1845-50	Mary Ann Norfolk.
1.51.	Ellen Osborn
1.53.	Susan Elliot.

Kitchen Maids

1.40.	Kezia Cream
1841-45	Sarah Elliot (Mrs Newman).
1845-46	Mary Pearson.
1846-48	Mary Reid.
1848-53	Sarah Hunt.

APPENDIX SIXTEEN

Servants of Mrs David Markham (After David Markham's Death)

Housekeepers

1853-55	Mary Patey. Formerly Mary Atkinson, cook at Horkesley from 1838-1853.
1.57.	Elizabeth Wise.

Housekeeper and Lady's Maid

1857-1867	Esther Cutler. In her service since 1849. After 1876 maid to Mrs Clements. Mrs Markham left her a legacy of £15.00 a year.

Young Lady's Maid

1.57.	Esther Cutler

Housemaids

1.54.	Harriet Elliott.
1.57.	Alice Mallinson
1859-60	Emily Polley. From Horkesley.
1864-73	Emelia Evers. Niece of Susan Elliot
1873-75	Sarah Burton. Niece of Esther Cutler.

Cooks

1.60.	Elizabeth Laramy. From Arlington.
1.64.	Mary Jane Boon.
1864-68	Elizabeth King.

1868-70	Phoebe Cresswell.
1870-75	Margaret Wallace. From Ashfield.

Kitchen Maids

1854-55	Tamar Minter. From Horkesley.
1855-56	Jane Eades.
1856-57	Emily Polley. From Horkesley.

Butlers

1853-55	James Patey
1855-56	Frederick Johnston
1856-57	Robert Houghton

APPENDIX SEVENTEEN

The Great Horkesley Infant School

The National School was built alongside the Infant School that had been established by David Markham. The Schoolmaster's house was also built close by, with the result that much of the Infant School playground was lost. The national school was run by a Mr Page, a trained teacher, with his wife, also a trained teacher, taking the Infant School. Their daughter was pupil teacher.

Average School Attendance:

1874.	- 39
1875.	- 77
1876.	- 79
1877.	- 86
1879.	- 89
1880.	- 97
1881	- 110

APPENDIX EIGHTEEN

Clergymen at Great Horkesley

Rectors	Curates	Date	Remarks
Dr. John Cock		1771	Also Vicar of Depden
Rev. Philip Yorke		1796	Prebendary of Ely
Dr. William Ward		1817	Bishop of Sodor and Man
	Rev. P. Ward	1819-21	
	Rev. Sir A. Hennehob	1829-33	
	Rev. James Crebbin	1833-38	
Rev. David Markham		1838	Canon of Windsor Rural Dean of Dedham
	Rev. C. Holland	1840-44	
	Rev. H.W. Baker	1844-51	
	Rev. W.H. Edwards	1851-53	
Rev. J.B. Magenis		1853	
	Rev. John Weir	1853-62	
Rev. John Steel		1862	
	Rev. J. Steel (Jun)	1863-69	
	Rev. D.E. Holland	1869-72	
	Rev. J. Harrison	1872-76	
Rev. John Storr		1876	Rural Dean of Dedham
	Rev. J. Triphook		

APPENDIX NINETEEN

Clergymen at Stillingfleet

Vicars	Curates	Date	Remarks
Rev. Thomas Eglin		1768	Vicar 50 years
Rev. A.J. Wm. Eyre		1818	Went to Horsey 1826
Rev. D.F. Markham		1826	Went to Horkesley 1838
	Rev. R.S. Bree	1831-36	
	Rev. D. Nelson	1836-37	
	Rev. T.G. Clay	1837-38	
Rev. Charles Hawkins		1838	Died in 1857
	Rev. J. Wood	1839-48	
	Rev. H.G. Pretyman	1848-51	
	Rev. John Baillie	1851-53	
	Rev. F.L. Lamotte	1853-57	
Rev. E.J. Raines		1857-59	Died May 30th. Buried at Stillingfleet, aged 49.
Rev. G. Hustler		1859-75	Retired to a villa in Oxfordshiret. Died hunting 1905, aged 79

	Rev. G.D. Armitage	1861-71
	Rev. R.W. Kemplay	
Rev. W.A. Wightman		1875-84
Rev. A. Grimston		1884-1914
Rev. Arthur F. Chappell		1914

APPENDIX TWENTY

Selected Works of Sir Clements Markham

Franklin's Footsteps (1852)

Travels in Peru and India (1862)

Cuzco. A Journey to the Ancient Capital of Peru. With an Account of the History, Language, Literature, and Antiquities of the Incas. And Lima. A Visit to the Capital and Provinces of Modern Peru (1856).

Voyages of Sir James Lancaster to the East Indies (1877)

(Trans.) Narrative of the Embassy of Ruy Gonzalez De Clavijo to the Court of Timour at Samarcand A.D. 1403-6 (1859)

On the Origins and Migrations of the Greenland Esquimaux (1865).

A Life of the Great Lord Fairfax (1870)

A Memoir on the Indian Surveys (1871)

Ollanta, a Quichua Drama (1871)

Railroad and Steam Communication in Southern Peru (1874).

Peru. With Illustrations (1880)

The Sea Fathers: Lives of Great Navigators of Former Times (1884)

A Life of John Davis, The Navigator, 1550-1605, Discoverer of David Straits (1889).

A History of Peru (1892).

Columbus, and the Fourth Centenary of His Discovery (1892).

Life of Captain Stephen Martin (1895)

The Antarctic Expeditions (1899)

Considerations Respecting Routes for an Antarctic Expedition (1901)

Antarctic Sledge Travelling (1903).

Commemoration of the Reign of Queen Elizabeth (1903)

C. Reginald Enock's Journeys in Peru (1905).

On the Next Great Arctic Discovery: The Beaufort Sea (1906)

Richard III: His Life & Character Reviewed in Light of Recent Research (1906)

King Edward VI an Appreciation (1908).

Admiral Sir Leopold MocLintock K.C.B. (1908)

The Incas of Peru (1910)

The Land of the Incas (1910)

The Conquest of New Granada (1912)

Vasco Nunez De Balboa, 1513-1913 (1913)

The Capture of Lima, 1881 (1914)

Narratives of the Mission of George Bogle to Tibet and the Journey of Thomas Manning to Lhasa (1877)

Scott's Last Expedition (1913).

The First Combat Between Modern Ironclads, 1879 (1914).

Early Voyages to the Strait of Magellan (1911)

(Edited by) The War of Quito and Incan Documents (1913)

Editor, Proceedings of the Royal Geographical Society, 1872-1878.

BIBLIOGRAPHY

Aston, Nigel, "Markham, William (bap. 1719, d.1807)" *Oxford Dictionary of National Biography*. Oxford: Oxford University Press, 2004. Online Ed.

Baigent, Elizabeth, "Markham, Sir Clements Robert (1830-1916), *Oxford Dictionary of National Biography*. Oxford: Oxford University Press, 2004. Online Ed.

Blanchard, Peter, (Ed.), *Markham in Peru: The Travels of Clements R. Markham, 1852-1853*. Austin: University of Texas Press, 1991.

Brown, Andrew, "Lytton, Edward George Earle Lytton Bulwer, first Baron Lytton (1803-1873)" *Oxford Dictionary of National Biography*. Oxford: Oxford University Press, 2004. Online Ed.

Brown, Lesley, (Ed.), *The New Shorter Oxford English Dictionary*. Vol.1 and 2. Oxford: Clarendon Press, 1993.

Burroughs, Peter, "Grey, Henry George, third Earl Grey (1802-1894)" *Oxford Dictionary of National Biography*. Oxford: Oxford University Press, 2004. Online Ed.

Buxton, Stephen, *Revolutions in the Earth*. London: Weidenfeld & Nicolson, 2003.

Callender, G.A.R., "Hamilton, Sir Richard Vesey (1829-1912)" *Oxford Dictionary of National Biography*. Oxford: Oxford University Press, 2004. Online Ed.

Cannon, John, (Ed.), *The Oxford Companion to British History.* Oxford: Oxford University Press, 2002.

Carlyle, E.I., "Vyse, Richard William Howard (1784-1853)" *Oxford Dictionary of National Biography*. Oxford: Oxford University Press, 2004. Online Ed.

Chamberlain, Muriel E., "Canning, Stratford, Viscount Stratford de Redcliffe (1786-1880) *Oxford Dictionary of National Biography*. Oxford: Oxford University Press, 2006. Online Ed.

Clerke, E.M., "Adelaide (1792-1849)" *Oxford Dictionary of National Biography*. Oxford: Oxford University Press, 2004. Online Ed.

Cliffe, J.T., "Danby Family (per. 1493-1667)" *Oxford Dictionary of National Biography*. Oxford: Oxford University Press, 2004. Online Ed.

Copsey, Richard, "Scrope, Thomas (d.1492)" *Oxford Dictionary of National Biography*. Oxford: Oxford University Press, 2004. Online Ed.

Dakin, D., *British and American Philhellenes During the Greek War of Independence, 1821-1833.*

De La Bedoyere, *Defying Rome*. Stroud: Tempus, 2003.

Donagan, Barbara, "Lucas, Sir Charles (1612/13-1648)" *Oxford Dictionary of National Biography*. Oxford: Oxford University press, 2004. Online Ed.

Drain, Susan, "Baker, Sir Henry Williams, third baronet (1821-1877)" *Oxford Dictionary of National Biography*. Oxford: Oxford University Press, 2004. Online Ed.

Fisher, D.R., "Griffin, Richard, third Baron Braybrooke (1783-1858)" *Oxford Dictionary of National Biography*. Oxford: Oxford University Press, 2004. Online Ed.

Foulkes, Richard, "Macready, William Charles (1793-1873)" *Oxford Dictionary of National Biography*. Oxford: Oxford University Press, 2004. Online Ed.

Gough, Barry, *The Royal Navy and the North-West Coast of North America 1810-1914: A Study.* 1971.

Gray, Jack, *Rebellions and Revolutions: China from the 1800s to 2000.* 2nd Ed. Oxford: Oxford University Press, 2002.

Hanes, W. Travis, Sanello, Frank, *The Opium Wars*. Illinois: Sourcebooks, Inc., 2002.

Hughes, Jonathan, "Vere, John de, sixteenth earl of Oxford (1516-1562)" *Oxford Dictionary of National Biography*. Oxford: Oxford University Press, 2004. Online Ed.

Hunt, William, "Hervey, Lord Arthur Charles (1808-1894)" *Oxford Dictionary of National Biography*. Oxford: Oxford University Press, 2004. Online Ed.

Jack, Sybil M., "Wolsey, Thomas (1470/71-1530)" *Oxford Dictionary of National Biography*. Oxford: Oxford University Press, 2004. Online Ed.

Lancaster, Charles, *Seeing England: Antiquaries, Travellers & Naturalists*. Chalford: Nonsuch Publishing, 2008.

Lane-Poole, Stanley, "Sir Richard Church (Continued) *The English Historical Review*. Vol. 5, No. 19 (Jul. 1890).

Laughton, J.K., "Glascock, William Nugent (1787?-1847)" *Oxford Dictionary of National Biography*. Oxford: Oxford University Press, 2004. Online Ed.

"Parker, Sir William, first baronet (1781-1866)" *Oxford Dictionary of National Biography*. Oxford: Oxford University Press, 2004. Online Ed.

"Seymour, Sir George Francis (1787-1870)" *Oxford Dictionary of National Biography*. Oxford: Oxford University Press, 2004. Online Ed.

Leapman, Michael, *Inigo*. London: Headline Books, 2004.

Levine, Philippa, "The Amatuer and the Professional: Antiquarians, Historians and Archaeologists in Victorian England, 1838-1886"

Lewis, M. *The Navy in Transition 1814-1864: A Social History*. 1965.

Lynch, Barbara D. and Lynch, Thomas F., "The Beginnings of a Scientific Approach to Prehistoric Archaeology in 17th and 18th Century Britain" *Southwestern Journal of Anthropology*. Vol. 24, No.1 (Spring, 1968).

McLean, David, "The Greek Revolutionand the Anglo-French Entent 1843-4" *The English Historical Review*. Vol. 96, No. 378 (Jan.1981).

Mitchell, Charles, *A Book of Ships*. Harmondsworth: Penguin, 1941.

Momigliano, Arnaldo, "Ancient History and the Antiquarian" *Journal of the Warburg and Courtauld Institutes*. Vol. 13, No. 3/4 (1950).

Nicholls, Mark, "Markham, Sir Griffin (b.c.1565, d. in or after 1644)" *Oxford Dictionary of National Biography*. Oxford: Oxford University Press, 2004.Online Ed.

Orbell, John, "Baring, Alexander, first Baron Ashburton (1773-1848)" *Oxford Dictionary of National Biography*. Oxford: Oxford University Press, 2004. Online Ed.

Paoletti, John T., Radke, Gary M., *Art in Renaissance Italy*. 2nd Ed. London: Laurence King Publishing, 2001.

Piggot, Stuart, *Ancient Britons and the Antiquarian Imagination*.

Prest, Wilfrid, "Winch, Sir Humphrey (1554/5-1625)" *Oxford Dictionary of National Biography*. Oxford: Oxford University Press, 2004. Online Ed.

Robinson, C.E., *A History of Greece*.

Schnapp, Alain, *The Discovery of the Past*

Stamp, Gavin, "Scott, Sir George Gilbert (1811-1878)" *Oxford Dictionary of National Biography*. Oxford: Oxford University Press, 2004. Online Ed.

Stater, Victor, "Vere, Aubrey de, twentieth earl of Oxford (1627-1703)" *Oxford Dictionary of National Biography*. Oxford: Oxford University Press, 2004. Online Ed.

St. Clair, William, *That Greece Might Still Be Free*.

Stephen, Leslie, "Goodall, Joseph (1760-1840)" *Oxford Dictionary of National Biography*. Oxford: Oxford University Press, 2006. Online Ed.

Stephens, H.M., "Church, Sir Richard (1784-1873)" *Oxford Dictionary of National Biography*. Oxford: Oxford University Press, 2004. Online Ed.

Syrett, David, and DiNando, R.L., *The Commissioned Sea Officers of the Royal Navy 1660-1815*. Aldershot: Scholar Press for the Society, 1994.

Temperley, H.W.V., "The Last Phase of Stratford de Redcliffe" *English Historical Review*. 47 (1932).

Vetch, R.H., "Galton, Sir Douglas Strutt (1822-1899)" *Oxford Dictionary of National Biography*. Oxford: Oxford University Press, 2005. Online Ed.

Wacher, John, *The Towns of Roman Britain*. 2nd Ed. London: B.T.Batsford, 1995.

Waite, John, *Boudica's Last Stand*. Stroud: The History Press, 2007

Wroth, W.W., "Mure, William (1799-1860)" *Oxford Dictionary of National Biography*. Oxford: Oxford University Press, 2006. Online Ed.

INDEX

Lightning Source UK Ltd.
Milton Keynes UK
UKHW010742070721
386761UK00001B/44